IMAGES
of America

LAKE ARROWHEAD
ARCHITECTURE

THE VILLAGE EVOLVES. At some point, the Village received stenciling on the walls of its buildings. By 1953, the Village was described as a Bavarian village rather than the "English/Norman" village the original descriptions touted. It is not entirely clear when this change in perception of the architecture of the Village occurred, but it was most likely influenced by the GIs returning from service in Europe during World War II. Over the years, the architecture of Lake Arrowhead took on its own stylistic characteristics, which can now be described as Old Arrowhead—a creative blend of English/French/Norman/Cottage/Swiss/Bavarian architecture. (John Lyles Collection.)

ON THE COVER: LAKE ARROWHEAD CONSERVATION RUN. This photograph shows the first annual Conservation Run, which took place on July 27, 1926. The run started at 6:00 a.m. at the Automobile Club of Southern California at Adams and Figueroa Streets in Los Angeles and ended by noon at the Lake Arrowhead Village. Awards were given to the three cars "using the least amount of gasoline, oil and water." This was determined by the following method: "The total weight of the car in tons times the number of miles driven, divided by the number of gallons of gasoline consumed. The result is ton miles per gallon of gasoline." Vehicle weight included the driver and no more than four passengers and 100 pounds of luggage. Gas, oil, and water tanks were to be filled to capacity at the beginning of the run. Upon arrival at Arrowhead the tanks were refilled and the amounts used recorded. Only nonprofessional drivers operating their own cars were allowed to enter. (Russ Keller Collection.)

IMAGES
of America

LAKE ARROWHEAD
ARCHITECTURE

Diane Wilk

ARCADIA
PUBLISHING

Copyright © 2023 by Diane Wilk
ISBN 978-1-4671-0965-9

Published by Arcadia Publishing
Charleston, South Carolina

Printed in the United States of America

Library of Congress Control Number: 2022951095

For all general information, please contact Arcadia Publishing:
Telephone 843-853-2070
Fax 843-853-0044
E-mail sales@arcadiapublishing.com
For customer service and orders:
Toll-Free 1-888-313-2665

Visit us on the Internet at www.arcadiapublishing.com

To my parents, Stefan and Wanda Wilk; to my husband, Michael Burch; to my children, James, Katherine, and Richard Burch; and to all who want to get to know more about our mountain home.

CONTENTS

ACKNOWLEDGMENTS

This book would not have been possible without the help of the following people: Russ Keller and Rhea-Frances Tetley, of the Rim of the World Historical Society, who had tremendous patience with me and helped me find all sorts of information I would not have otherwise found; John Dahl, an invaluable source of information on the history of Lake Arrowhead; John Lyles, fellow architect and collector extraordinaire, who helped find many of the historical photographs from his personal collection; Putty Henck, for personally telling me stories about growing up on the mountain; Joey Arbegue; Dee Carawan, AIA; Lisa and Barry Daily; Jeff Dierksmeier; Ron Dolman; April and Tricia DuFour; Chris Dunn; Mike Feddersen; Kelli Flint; Carolyn Fox; Prof. Mark Gelernter; Lan Gerard; Nathan Gonzales; Tony Gonzales; Jim Grant; Peter Henck; Josh Karela; Glen Keane; Linda Kelter; Bernie Kerkvliet; Prof. Gary McGavin, AIA; Rusty McGuire; Vince Moses; Bill and Melinda Patton; Patrick Patton; Sue Payne; David Pickard, Esq., AIA; Bill Pumford; Debra Salinas; Ann Scheid; Shelly and Mark Scott; Julie Shanahan; Gerald Shingleton; James Tang; Ted Thomas; David and Cindy Vail; Daniela Holt Voith, FAIA; and Ingrid Wicken. Also, all the folks at Arcadia Publishing, especially senior title manager Caitrin Cunningham, who helped make this book a reality. I cannot forget my kids for enjoying my relating the stories to them, my husband for supporting me in this endeavor and looking forward to exploring and finding houses to put in the book, and last but not least, my parents, Stefan and Wanda Wilk, who first introduced me to the mountain. If I forgot anyone, I apologize for the oversight.

The following abbreviations are used in courtesy lines throughout the book:

A&A: *Arts & Architecture*
AD&A: University of California, Santa Barbara, Art, Design & Architecture Museum
AKSL: Photo Courtesy A.K. Smiley Library
AL: Alamy
BC: Bob Compere
BP: Bill Pumford Collection
CD: Chris Dunn
CF: Carolyn Fox
CSL-FM: California State Library, Frederick W. Martin, Photographer, SoCal Digitation Project
DC: Dee Carawan
DP: David Pickard
DS: Debra Salinas
DV: David Vail
DW: Diane Wilk Collection
GK: Glen Keane
LA-GRI: Lautner Archive, Research Library, Getty Research Institute, LA © 2022 The John Lautner Foundation
GRI: © J. Paul Getty Trust. Getty Research Institute, Los Angeles (2004.R.10)
HL: Huntington Library
MSP: Josh Karela, Mountain Shutter Photography
JG: John Gerard
JL: John Lyles Collection
JS: Julie Shanahan
JT: James Tang Photographer

KSL: Ingrid P. Wicken, California Ski Library
LG: Lan Gerard
LAPL-LPC: Los Angeles Public Library–Photographers Collection (C.C. Pierce)
LAT: *Los Angeles Times*
LBD: Lisa and Barry Daily
LOC: Library of Congress
M: Mozumdar.org
MAHF: Malibu Adamson House Foundation Archives
MF: Mike Feddersen
MSS: Mark and Shelly Scott
PH: Putty Henck Collection
PP: Patrick Patton
RD: Ron Dolman
RK: Russ Keller Collection
ROWHS: Rim of the World Historical Society
RT: Rhea-Frances Tetley Collection
SBCM: San Bernardino County Museum
SBCL: San Bernardino County Library
SL: Sherman Library
SPS: Steele's Photo Service
UCLA-BP: Adelbert Bartlett Papers, UCLA Library Special Collections, Charles E. Young Research Library
USC-AFAL: USC Art and Fine Arts Library
USCL-CHS: USC Libraries, California Historical Society

INTRODUCTION

Who would have thought that a sleepy little mountain town—with a public face that consists of a few outlet stores and restaurants surrounded by a sea of cars—would boast one of Southern California's richest concentrations of buildings by significant 20th-century architects? Yet here we are. Amongst the most important and influential architects practicing in Southern California during the early part of the 20th century are the following names: John Byers, AIA; Stiles O. Clements, AIA; Roland Coate, FAIA; Robert Farqhuar, FAIA; Reginald Johnson, FAIA; Gordon Kaufman, FAIA; John Lautner, FAIA; Elda Muir, AIA; Wallace Neff, FAIA; Garrett Van Pelt, FAIA; Lloyd Wright; William Woollett, FAIA; and, of course, Paul Revere Williams, FAIA, and Richard Neutra, FAIA—both AIA Gold Medalists. All of these architects (and more) designed buildings in Lake Arrowhead. Even Lutah Maria Riggs, FAIA, is said to have designed a house (the Lockwood Cabin) in Lake Arrowhead, but both the location and confirmation that it was actually built remain elusive. These were the "starchitects"—a portmanteau used to describe architects whose celebrity and critical acclaim have transformed them into idols of the architecture world and may even have given them some degree of fame among the general public—of their time and made an indelible mark on the built environment of Los Angeles in the early 20th century. In Lake Arrowhead, perhaps the only familiar name on that list is Paul Revere Williams, who built quite a few projects in Arrowhead, including the Lake Arrowhead Community Presbyterian Church. However, many of the architects on the list built more houses in the community than Williams, but today, few people remember that they did.

It is highly unusual to have such a concentration of famous designers/architects working in one place. During the 1920s, the area was difficult to get to and considered a hideaway for Southern California's rich and famous. It is not surprising that the architects who were hired to build getaways for celebrity clients might have wanted to keep the location and projects secret. The quality of the early-20th-century architecture in Lake Arrowhead is astounding, and some digging into its provenance brought to light an amazing architectural pedigree.

The book is divided into the following sections: the Pragmatists, Romantics, Mythmakers, Escapists, Modernists, and Dreamers. Each of these categories expresses the zeitgeist of their respective time. The history dates to long before Lake Arrowhead was even recognized as a place, back 1,200 years or more, with the Indigenous people who once called the mountain home. I discuss the various periods of building on the mountain, ranging from when it was simply a place to exploit to the present time, when it is more of a place to dream. I give examples of buildings during the various time periods and also try to explain why they look the way they do. Please note that there are so many great houses on the mountain, and if I have not mentioned yours, it does not mean it was not worthy of inclusion in this book.

Chapter one is devoted to the mountain before Lake Arrowhead even existed. I never knew the complete story—and I still do not, but what I do know is fascinating. This is the story of the tragedy of the decimation of the native population of the United States, the Wild West, great fortunes made and lost, industrialization, trains, the Victorian Age, and the beginnings of the environmental conservation movement. In short, it offers a picture of the story of the United States of America, all here on our local mountain. In terms of architecture, the trees that were logged were used for making crates to ship citrus farmed in the San Bernardino Valley to all around the country and for structures such as the Morey Mansion, built in 1890 in Redlands, a great Victorian house known by names such as the Orange Empire House and America's Favorite Victorian. Another example is the Edwards Mansion, also built in 1890. Because of the citrus industry and the ability to distribute goods via railroad, the San Bernardino Valley became the richest (per capita) region in the country at the beginning of the 20th century. Just a few years later, more eclectic revivals became the rage, as shown by buildings such as Kimberly Crest (dating from 1897) and the A.K. Smiley Library (built in 1898) in Redlands. These Victorians chose another way of building altogether on the mountain. To understand why, one needs to recognize the changes occurring across the country at the time.

In 1885, the southern leg of the transcontinental railroad line reached the San Bernardino Valley. Shortly thereafter, in 1890, an official announcement was made that the American frontier was closed. This told many educated Americans that natural resources and land were not inexhaustible. It is with this realization that chapter two begins. Until this time, the wilderness was often considered something to be tamed and civilized. Around 1890, the conservation movement began and sought to preserve and protect the wildlife, wildlands, and other natural resources of the continent. Writings by people such as John Burroughs, George Perkins Marsh, John Muir, Gifford Pinchot, John Wesley Powell, and Henry David Thoreau argued for environmental protections and the conservation of natural resources. As industrialization caused cities to become more and more crowded and polluted, those who could started to look for ways of getting out of the cities to find peaceful retreats. Camping, birdwatching, fishing, and other outdoor activities became popular pastimes for those who could afford to get away. Books like *Wild Northern Scenes: Sporting Adventures with the Rifle and the Rod* by S.H. Hammond (1857) offer an example of a work that promoted the connection between recreation and preservation. People also started to become aware of wild lands when explorers brought back images of what they had seen on them. Books such as *Picturesque America* (1872), with images of the spectacular scenery of the frontier, wowed people and helped them appreciate the natural wonders throughout the country. Of course, the rise of industrialization and the ease of being able to get to these once remote places by train opened up the country so more people could see these wonders for themselves. It is not surprising that Yellowstone National Park was founded in 1872, followed by Yosemite and Sequoia National Parks in 1890. The National Park Service was established in 1916.

This appreciation of the wilderness and nature was not limited to the United States. Proto-environmentalism was on the rise in places such as England. Writer John Ruskin critiqued industrialization and emphasized the connections between nature, art, and society. A recent Harvard University Library Colloquium on Proto-Environmentalism held a session entitled "Green Sage: John Ruskin as Proto-Environmentalist" and described the session as such: "The Victorian polymath John Ruskin (1819–1900) was among the earliest to recognize the threat posed by industrial and anthropogenic pollutants to the natural world." Others, such as William Morris, pushed to protect the natural world from the ravages of pollution and industrialization, causing some historians of the Green movement to regard Morris as an important forerunner. Author Patrick O'Sullivan states, "[I]n NEWS FROM NOWHERE [sic] (1890), Morris anticipated many aspects of modern green thought – alternative technology, renewable energy, simplicity of lifestyle, community self-reliance, production only for need, prolonging the life of goods in order to reduce resource depletion, reduction of waste, and above all the key role of what is defined as 'work' (for both men and women) in allowing us all to express our essential humanity in a free and sustainable society." These proto-environmentalists helped set the stage for the current Green movement. Of note is that both Ruskin and Morris were revolutionary socialists. Although the Progressive movement in the United States did embrace this thinking, most Americans rejected the socialist aspect of environmentalism, keeping only the emotional/romanticized response to the environment and individualism of the Romantics. In fact, wealthy industrialists and capitalists embraced the movement, seeing that it was another way of making money by bringing tourists to the wilderness via a new means of transportation made possible by industrialization—trains. Trains even played a role on the mountain in Lake Arrowhead. The writings of Ruskin and Morris most likely would have been known to those interested in the conservation of the wilderness.

The Arts and Crafts movement expressed concerns about industrialization. This led to a re-evaluation of handcrafts and a romanticization of precapitalist forms of culture and society, as well as an architecture that glorified and romanticized nature. Note the formation of Arts and Crafts societies across the country, including Gustav Stickley's Arts and Crafts furniture company, founded in 1883, and the artisan community of Roycroft, founded in 1895. The first Arts and

Crafts Society in the United States was founded in 1897, closely followed by Chicago's Arts and Crafts Society that began that same year.

What is normally associated with the American Arts and Crafts movement was not the only architectural trend influenced by the writings of Morris and Ruskin. The architecture of the American wilderness was also heavily influenced by them. In the Adirondacks, this showed up as part of the movement of wealthy city dwellers getting away from the hustle and bustle of urban industrialized life. The Great Camps of the Adirondacks, a rustic architecture built from locally obtained materials, were meticulously handcrafted. It is often said that this architecture was influenced in part by the Swiss Chalet architecture championed by A.J. Downing in his influential 1850 book *The Architecture of Country Houses* but also by traditional Japanese architecture— something that designers became aware of after the opening of Japan to the Western world in 1853. W.W. Durant is credited with the first Great Camp, Camp Pine Knot, which was completed in 1877.

Dude ranches, with a similar rustic architecture, started being opened around 1893, partly in reaction to the Panic of 1893, during which ranchers needed to find other sources of income and so opened their holdings to wealthy tourists who arrived by train. Teddy Roosevelt was probably the most famous of the "dudes." The architecture of the first dude ranches was initially the actual frontier buildings found on ranches, with later versions playing up the Romantic ideals of the Western Myth. The heyday of these dude ranches was in the 1920s. Part of the same trend are the great Western lodges of the National Park System, featuring architecture sometimes now affectionately dubbed "Parkitecture." The first of these grand lodges is Old Faithful Inn, built in 1904 in Yellowstone Park. As with the architecture of the Adirondacks, the structures in some national parks romanticized the wilderness and used natural materials found on the site. This is a more rustic version of the Arts and Crafts movements than, say, the refined Arts and Crafts architecture of Greene and Greene, as shown in their masterpiece, Pasadena's Gamble House of 1908, or the carefully crafted furnishings of Gustav Stickley. The architecture in the San Bernardino Mountains was not very different, in terms of inspiration, from the architecture of the Adirondacks, the dude ranches, or the later Parkitecture. However, they were different from the pragmatic structures of the logging mills that were completely utilitarian in function and had dotted the landscape for the first 40 or so years since people began streaming to the frontier from further east. The earliest of these camps, such as the Squirrel Inn and Pinecrest, romanticized the forests and the wilderness, taking their cues from the writings of influential architectural theorists of the time, including Ruskin, Morris, and A.W.N. Pugin.

The start of the 20th century brought in new ideas about what constituted good design. The chaotic nature of Victorian architecture, with its multitude of styles and variations, gave way to a new architectural quest of finding a more unified design strategy. These modern architects followed two major trends—those who looked toward historical precedents for inspiration and those who tried to find universal truths in abstraction. In Southern California, many architects looked toward Mediterranean and Spanish precedents for inspiration because of the topography and climate. That did not seem appropriate for the mountains, and French/Norman precedents became a more common inspiration for these designs. Rudolf Schindler, a European transplant, brought a more abstract form of modernism to the mountains with his design of what some have dubbed the world's first modern A-frame house right here in Arrowhead.

Chapters three, four, and five discuss "Old Arrowhead" architecture, which is based on European historical precedent but modified to fit Hollywood's conception of what constituted Anglo/French/Norman architecture. This is the period when the myth began to form around what Old Arrowhead is considered to be and is often referred to as Arrowhead's Golden Age. The architecture of this period is not really a copy of what would have been built in Europe; it is a fanciful, much more theatrical and innovative style than anything that could be found in the Old World, and it is an eclectic, modern and creative blend of styles unique to Lake Arrowhead.

Chapters six and seven also center on Arrowhead's Golden Age, but I have chosen to refer to this period as belonging to the Escapists. The movies, which offered so much escape from the Great Depression, played an oversized role in the creation of Lake Arrowhead. I discuss the influence of the movies on the architecture and the various entertainment and resort venues built in the area during this time, including the homes built by the many aviators who made money during World War II by "escaping" into the skies and then to their mountain retreats.

Chapters eight and nine discuss the Modernists and the new way of looking at architecture that was so prevalent during the middle of the 20th century in America. This is not to say that the Old Arrowhead architecture was not essentially and fully modern—it was. It is just that the more abstracted modern style took on a more prominent position in design strategies at this time. As obscure as Arrowhead may be to those outside Southern California, Arrowhead played an important role in the development of modern architecture.

In chapter ten, I close the book with a look at the state of building today in Lake Arrowhead and the role of fantasy and romance in the current trends on the mountain. I do not know where we go from here, but if history is any indication, I'm sure we are on the cusp of new and exciting things happening to the built environment on the mountain. The first break came in the 1890s with the closing of the frontier, the second came after World War I and the Spanish Flu pandemic, and the third came after the Great Depression and World War II. We are in the middle of another life-changing, worldwide pandemic. I can already sense changes in the demographics of the mountain community I grew up in. It will be interesting to see where we go from here. Hopefully, I will provide a bit of insight into where we have been so the generations that come after can make informed decisions about where they want this mountain community to go next.

This book offers readers a glimpse into some of Lake Arrowhead's history and the homes and buildings that still bring delight and amazement to their owners. Due to limitations of space in the book and time to do the research, not every incredible building on the mountain is included. This is a work in progress. It has been a fun adventure researching and thinking about the architecture of Lake Arrowhead, and I hope you enjoy reading what I have put together.

—Diane Wilk, AIA
Lake Arrowhead

One

THE PRAGMATISTS
IN THE BEGINNING

HUCKLEBERRY FINN.

THE QUINTESSENTIAL
PRAGMATIST. According to
Mark Twain's quintessential
pragmatist, Huckleberry
Finn, "anything is right,
good, or true if it works
adequately." The first
building on the mountain
certainly reflected this
philosophy. From the
Indigenous peoples who
took shelter in temporary
structures to the Mormon
settlers and loggers, there
was no time or resources
available for the luxury
of anything more. Even
the railroad tracks on the
mountain followed this
maxim. (LOC.)

THE INDIGENOUS INHABITANTS. Lake Arrowhead's Indigenous inhabitants called themselves Yuhaviatam, meaning "people of the pines." Spanish explorers named them Serrano, meaning "mountain people." Archeological evidence dates habitation in the area around Lake Arrowhead to between 500 and 1,200 years ago. A few rock paintings and some mortar holes in the granite are the only visible remaining evidence. The closest archaeological site is Rock Camp, about three miles north of the lake. (DW.)

SERRANO HOUSES. The Indigenous inhabitants lived in semisubterranean houses called *kiich*, measuring 12 to 14 feet across. They were built of stick frames covered in brush and latched together with yucca fiber. The mountains were used in the summer and fall for hunting and gathering piñon nuts and acorns. By the time the first Europeans arrived, few Indigenous people remained, as they had either been driven away from their ancestral homes or decimated by disease. (LOC.)

THE "DISCOVERY," 1776. In March 1776, a Spanish priest, Francisco Tomas Germenegildo Garces (b. 1738), passed through the mountains on his way to Mission San Gabriel led by a group of Mojave Indians. He was perhaps the first nonnative person to step foot in the area now known as Lake Arrowhead. It was not until 1826, however, that Little Bear Valley was "discovered" by a fur trader and partner of the explorer Jedediah Smith on the first overland trip to the California Coast. In 1850, just 24 years after Smith's arrival, California became a state. Two years later, in 1852, Mormon settlers built the first road up to the crest of the mountain from the San Bernardino Valley. Smith's excursion is memorialized in this painting by Frederick Remington that dates from 1906 and is titled *Jedediah Smith's Party Crossing the burning Mojave Desert*. This image originally appeared in *Collier's* magazine in 1906. (LOC.)

THE MORMON ERA, 1851–1857. After California became a state in 1850, Brigham Young eyed the new state as the perfect immigration and mail stop between Salt Lake and San Pedro. He purchased the entire Rancho San Bernardino from the Lugo family at the base of the mountain and sent 150 covered wagons with 500 settlers to form Southern California's first Anglo settlement. They named their new settlement San Bernardino. (LAPL-LC.)

MILL CREEK SAWMILL, 1850S. The new Mormon settlement that started in 1852 needed lumber, so eyeing the abundant virgin forests on the mountain, they built a road to the crest. It was completed in two and a half weeks. By 1854, there were six operational sawmills on the mountain. In 1857, Brigham Young recalled the settlers back to Utah. The 1857 Fort Tejon earthquake, which registered a 7.9 on the Richter scale, convinced the remaining Mormon settlers to return to Utah. (LAPL-CCP.)

LOGGING, 1853–1890. Early logging on the mountain was done by hand, as the modern chainsaw was not invented until the 1920s, and industrialized wood production with standardized sizes did not begin until around 1870. Logging was a noisy affair, with steam-driven engines and screeching circular saws in the mills. Bawling oxen and creaking wagons making their way down the mountain added to the chaos. (RK.)

PYGMY CABIN, HOLCOMB VALLEY, MID-1800S. Nicknamed the "Pygmy Cabin" for its six-foot-high ceiling and four-foot-tall door, this miner's cabin is typical of early mountain structures. Unfortunately, the Pygmy Cabin burned down in 1983. Log cabins were fast, easy, and cheap to assemble. The first log cabins in America can be traced to Swedish immigrants in the 1750s. (RK.)

CATTLE, 1860s–1950s. Ranching was an important part of the mountain economy, as there was an abundance of grass and water in the mountain meadows during the summer. In the late 1800s, there may have been as many as 1,000 head of cattle on the mountain. Ranching initially started to supply loggers and miners with food but later expanded to help mitigate severe drought in the high desert. As development increased in the mountains during the 1930s and 1940s, ranching declined accordingly. The creation of the many lakes on the mountain also reduced the amount of available grazing area. This drawing from 1870 shows cattle grazing in Little Bear Valley and looks toward the Talmadge/Benson Mill, which is now under Meadow Bay. Cowboys were often recruited for roles in the many Westerns that were filmed on the mountain. Changes in the US Forest Service grazing regulations also reduced the number of livestock that could be grazed, leading to the demise of ranching on the mountain. (SPS.)

KUFFEL HOMESTEAD, 1890s. In 1890, the Kuffel brothers, Adam and Frank, purchased the old Sherman-Metcalf Sawmill site and created a home from the old sawmill buildings. Historical accounts speak of beautiful gardens of flowers and apple trees in the fields around their home. In 1896, Adam Kuffel relinquished rights to part of the holdings to pay for his 15-year-old son's funeral; he had been found badly mauled by wild animals. In 1902, the Kuffel home burned in a wildfire, so they purchased Mangus Hansen's old house, which overlooked the valley (as shown here), for about $60. The original Kuffel house/Metcalf sawmill was located on the current site of Lady Bug Pond in Skypark at Santa's Village. The buildings on the Kuffel homestead, like the sawmills, were pragmatic structures. The Kuffels reportedly left the mountain by 1910. (Both, PH.)

BROOKINGS LUMBER AND BOX COMPANY NARROW-GAUGE RAILWAY, 1900–1913. With logging came the trains. Originally planned to go from the crest to the valley below, the line was only completed along the crest for hauling lumber to the mills. Forest preservation groups stopped the right-of-way to the valley. Brookings employed three Shay engines hauled to the crest by oxen. The lines were abandoned once they were no longer needed. The trains pulled rolling stock used for the transportation of logs. They did not transport people on these lines, however, as the tracks were hastily built by loggers and too unstable for the transportation of passengers. Derailments occurred, as shown here. The rail lines extended from Heaps Peak to Green Valley and were abandoned when Brookings moved to Oregon and founded the town of Brookings, Oregon. (Above, RK; below, AKSL.)

ARROWHEAD INCLINE, 1906/1907. The Arrowhead Reservoir and Power Company attempted to build an incline railway to help bring supplies up the mountain. Unfortunately, technical difficulties made the project untenable. James Mooney, who took over control of the operations of the company in 1905, was familiar with inclines, having owned another in Cincinnati. Started in 1906, the project ceased operation by 1907. There had been talk of turning the incline into a passenger line running from the Arrowhead Springs Hotel to the resorts on the mountain, but the line was not graded for passenger travel. Henry Huntington toyed with the idea of connecting the Pacific Electric network with his San Bernardino line and running it to the mountain resorts via the incline but realized it was not feasible. A major wildfire in 1911 irreparably damaged the already abandoned incline and ended any hope of a passenger line up the mountain. The Arrowhead Incline had an elevation gain of 1,769 feet and was 4,170 feet long. (RK.)

LITTLE BEAR DAM, 1891–1915. This photograph of the construction of Little Bear Dam shows one of the engines that was employed to build the dam. In total, three engines were brought up Waterman Canyon by being disassembled at the bottom of the grade and reassembled once they reached the dam site. Teams of 12 to 14 horses were said to have brought these locomotives up the mountain. The narrow-gauge engines did not always run smoothly and earned various nicknames in the process, such as "Leapin' Lena," "Whistling Billy," and other unprintable nicknames. The first locomotive, brought up in 1905, was named "Black Annie" because of the engine's supposed "feminine temperament." In addition to the locomotives, "four miles of steel rail, 45 dump cars, a steam hammer and two steam shovels" were employed. The photograph at left shows the completed outlet tower in 1904 while the lake was being filled. (Above, RK; left, SL.)

BLACK ANNIE, 1905–1915. This picture shows locomotive No. 1 (aka "Black Annie") after the engine was abandoned. After it was retired, the engine was placed on a short piece of track on a steep hill, where it was left on display for several decades before being moved to the Village as a tourist attraction. After it disappeared from the display at Lake Arrowhead, a rumor started to spread that it had been dumped in the bottom of the lake. In fact, it was taken by Jim Fouch, who displayed it at his hotel in Palm Springs, the La Pat Guest Ranch. Several owners and restorations later, Bob Walton of San Marino purchased the engine and restored it. Wanting to return the engine to its original working location, he transferred ownership to the Nevada State Railroad Museum in Carson City, Nevada, where it is displayed as the *Joe Douglass* (its original name). The engine was built in 1882 for the Dayton, Sutro & Carson Valley Railroad. (RK.)

HENCK HOMESTEAD, 1923. In 1923, Joseph Henck, an olive farmer from Hemet, and his wife, Mary Putnam, a UC Berkeley graduate active in the Hemet Ramona Festival, purchased the Kuffel homestead. They were part of a group of developers who purchased 400 acres in the Skyforest area in 1918 for $10,000 and developed the community of Skyforest, which was known as Forest of the Sky prior to 1928. Kuffel's Hansen Cabin is shown in 1904 (above) and in 1930 after the Hencks expanded it (below). The Hencks also brought electricity to their home and to Skyforest. Mary Putnam Henck founded the first school on the mountain. Her son, Joseph Putnam "Putty" Henck, also a UC Berkeley graduate, was a significant player in the development of Skyforest and, later, Santa's Village. After Putty Henck passed away in 2010, the property was sold and has since been remodeled yet again. (Both, PH.)

Two

THE ROMANTICS
THE ROMANCE OF THE MOUNTAINS

THE FIRST TOURISTS. The first sweet citrus was planted in San Bernardino in 1857, and by 1875 the first small orange grove was planted. Transcontinental train service reached San Bernardino in 1883, and in 1889 the first fruit from California was shipped to New York in a refrigerated car. Because of the explosion of the citrus industry, by 1895 Riverside was the wealthiest city per capita in the nation, and by 1900 there were 5,648,714 under cultivation! The wealthy ranchers wanted a playground to get away from the hot summers, and the mountains became their escape. Wilderness clubs were all the rage, and the wilderness experience was romanticized. Though the mountains could be difficult to access, tourists flocked to them. (SPS.)

SQUIRREL INN, 1892. The brainchild of James Mooney, the capitalist behind the Arrowhead Reservoir Company, the Squirrel Inn was the first of many clubs started in the San Bernardino Mountains in the late 19th century. In 1889, five investors purchased 160 acres near Strawberry Flat (now Twin Peaks). Membership was exclusive, with initiation fees costing almost a year's salary (for most people). A popular novel by Frank Stockton provided inspiration for name of the club. The "Change the Squirrel Event," which happened every fall, was the big social happening of the year at the Squirrel Inn. A stuffed squirrel, which adorned the signpost, was retired at the dinner. The following spring, a new squirrel would be shot, stuffed, and stuck on the sign. The below image shows retired squirrels (dating from 1893 to 1905) adorning the top of a log. (Both, RK.)

ADOLF WOOD CABIN AND NEW LODGE. Some of the cabins at the Squirrel Inn were so large that they could be considered inns in their own right. Local high rollers all had cabins, and members debated and planned the future of the mountain community. The original main lodge building burned down in 1922 but was rebuilt. In 1988, the Church of Spiritual Technology (CST) acquired the property. It is currently not open to the public. However, several of the original buildings can be seen from Highway 189 as it branches off from Highway 18. The above photograph shows Adolph Wood's cabin, which is still visible from Highway 189. Wood was vice president of the Arrowhead Reservoir Company and the on-site manager until his death in 1900. Below is the interior of one of the Squirrel Inn cabins with members of the Sunset Club playing cards. (Above, SBCM; below, USCL-CHS.)

PINE CREST/PINECREST, 1909. Dr. R. John Baylis was to San Bernardino what John Muir was to Yosemite. In 1904, when Baylis, a Squirrel Inn devotee, found out that the land immediately adjacent to the Squirrel Inn was available, he purchased those 160 acres to save the timber. Construction started by 1906, and the site eventually contained a dance pavilion, a café, a lounge, numerous cabins, a pool, and other recreational facilities. The advent of transcontinental rail tourism spiked interest in Native American crafts. The below image shows a collection of Native American baskets hanging from the ceiling of Pinecrest's lobby. Traders with federally issued licenses ran the business of the crafts trade, even dictating how and what each tribe would make. Previously, items such as these had been produced by the tribes for personal use. (Both, DW.)

THE ROOKERY AT PINECREST, 1917. This building at Pine Crest was called the Rookery and was most likely named after the definition meaning "a colony of breeding animals, generally reserved for a colony of gregarious birds" and not the one that describes dense slum housing in 19th-century London. The spelling of Pine Crest's name was eventually changed to Pinecrest. The Rookery was completed in 1917 but razed in 1967 after it was deemed a safety hazard—a fate that befell many of Pinecrest's other buildings. At one point, Pinecrest had been the largest public resort in the San Bernardino Mountains. The romanticization of nature is certainly apparent in the design of this staircase (probably located in the Rookery, which was reputed to have had a circular set of stairs). (Above, DW; right, JL.)

PINECREST LOOKOUT (ABOVE) AND GAME ROOM (LEFT). The lookout displayed a perfect mesh of modern and romantic attitudes toward nature. The large glass windows offered a viewing space inside the building, and the elaborate railing made from tree branches emphasizes its romanticization of nature. The game room featured a pool room downstairs and a card room upstairs and was relatively straightforward except that the designer chose to batter the exterior profile, adding visual weight to the structure. This simple design choice makes it appear as though the building is growing from the ground—another subtle nod to romantic notions about nature at the time. It was condemned by San Bernardino County in the 1990s and taken down. (Above, JL; left, DW.)

ROCKWOOD LODGE, 1915–1920.
Rockwood Lodge was designed and built by A.E. Scoles, a retired civil engineer once employed by John D. Rockefeller. Scoles wanted to replicate lodges that he remembered from growing up in Scandinavia. To that end, he employed traditional Norse building techniques, such as boiling the wood in oil to prevent rot and termite infestations and forcing worms under the bark to create patterns in the wood. The structure is made using exclusively local materials, which Scoles meticulously documented, claiming that "every wood in the mountains is represented in the edifice." The US Forest Service called Rockwood "the most unique building of its type in the entire United States." After Scoles sold the property, the new owner added gas, electricity, and phone service. After restoration, Rockwood Lodge was opened to the public in 2018 as part of Rockwood Cabins. (Both, DW.)

LITTLE BEAR LAKE RESORT, 1900s. A 1913 court decision precluded the use of the water for irrigation ending a years-long court battle over water rights from the lake, so the focus shifted to using the lake for recreation. As early as 1910, a Los Angeles Times article—headlined "Hip, Hip! Fishing at Little Bear"—announced a "Resort to be Started on Mountain Lake." James Mooney wanted to make the lake a private fishing club, but so many fishermen showed up on opening day in 1915 that extensive damage was done to the existing facilities. The Arrowhead Reservoir and Power Company temporarily closed Little Bear Lake, reopening it several weeks later with new concessions, including boat and tent rentals and a lunchroom. One and a half miles of shoreline were opened to the public, and the resort began to charge parking fees. (Both, RK.)

LITTLE BEAR LAKE POST OFFICE AND CABINS. In 1916, Little Bear Lake Resort had five miles of shoreline available for fishing and a 150-room hotel with extra tent cabins. By 1919, the resort boasted a pavilion, a lunchroom, 26 cabins, a post office, and boat rentals. It was even claimed that the lunch counter was "the longest in the state." Little Bear Lake Resort had become one of the most popular spots in the San Bernardino Mountains. Photographs of the resort show that it was architecturally similar to Pinecrest. The exterior of the post office used logs that still had their bark (right), and handrails on the cabins (below) were constructed from natural-looking branches. The structures emphasized and celebrated the rustic nature of the setting and presented a stark contrast to the high-style village that would be built on the same site three years later. (Right, DW; below, RK.)

THE PACIFIC ELECTRIC MAGAZINE

Vol. 12   LOS ANGELES, CAL., JULY 10, 1927   No. 2

The Portal to "Happy-Land"—The Pacific Electric Camp.

PACIFIC ELECTRIC COMPANY CAMP, 1917–1942. In 1915, the Pacific Electric Company purchased 20 acres near Lake Arrowhead as a vacation resort for its employees. It opened in 1917 with a large dining hall, a club room, a swimming pool, cottages, and a boat, the *Lady Louise*, that offered rides on Lake Arrowhead. Motor coach service was provided from downtown Los Angeles to the camp. The camp was exclusive to employees of the railway and only opened to the public after it was sold in 1942 to Leonard "Skipper" and Margery Steimle. The Steimles renamed the camp Beverly Pines and catered to families. Their camp slogan was "Children Preferred." In 1944, the name of the camp was changed to Pine View Lodge. The camp closed in 1974 after Skipper Steimle died. All that remains of the camp are the stone foundations, fireplace, and chimney. (Left, DW; below, JL.)

In Social Hall
Pacific Electric Vacation Home
San Bernardino Mountains

THE RAVEN HOTEL, 1919. Sisters Ann Copeland and Mabel Leonard built the Raven Hotel as a three-story, 28-room facility. They later added a 60-person dining room and extra lodging. After they died, Copeland's son George took over operations in 1943. When George died in 1951, it was sold to Elmer Luther, who expanded the hotel, renaming it the Arrowhead Inn and Cottages. It was sold again in the early 1980s and later renamed the Saddleback Inn. (RK.)

RESTAURANT, EARLY 1900S. Originally built as an entertainment establishment for loggers, this building housed a bar and dining area on the first two floors with a boudoir for social visits on the top floor. Its stained-glass windows and entry doors came from the 1860 Nevada State Capitol building, and an 80-foot bar came from the Ormsby House Hotel in Carson City, Nevada. A 2005 fire destroyed the stained glass and front door, but the bar was salvaged; it reopened in 2006. (DP.)

KAKI'S KABIN, 1924/1925.
Originally built for Karl and
Jane Thurston, this was one
of the first cabins built in
Skyforest. It is also now the last
remaining property holding on
the mountain that belongs to
the Henck family. This is a late
example of the rustic romantic
building style so prevalent on
the mountain around the start
of the 20th century with its
stone walls and natural wood
elements. It was purchased by
Catherine "Kaki" Henck Lovell
in 1968. She had her brother,
contractor Putty Henck, and
architect Atilla Batar double the
size of cabin, adding a master
suite and new kitchen in the
style of the original cabin.
(Both, DW.)

Three

THE MYTHMAKERS
ARROWHEAD'S GOLDEN AGE

A NEW VISION. The Arrowhead Lake Company purchased the lake with plans to convert the rustic Little Bear Lake Resort into "one of California's finest resorts." The company hired architect McNeal Swasey, who sought a calm, unified design strategy over Victorian exuberance. A contemporaneous critique of his work stated, "All were impressed with the orderly growth, the unifying architecture, the combination of the work of nature with artistic and beautiful works of man." (RK.)

THE CLUBHOUSE, 1922. Among the first buildings constructed by the Arrowhead Lake Company was a clubhouse on the North Shore where the company could entertain prospective property buyers. It has been said that construction began on the clubhouse in 1921 with McNeal Swasey as architect. The above photograph dates from 1927, and below is a 1932 postcard that shows the addition of a more extensive second floor designed by Roland Coate. In the 1940s, buildings were added to the tavern, including Cedar Lodge, which was built to house employees of the tavern, many of whom were seasonal; they lived in Palm Springs during the winter and moved to the mountain for the cooler summer months. (Both, RK.)

THE NORTH SHORE TAVERN. Initially, there were no roads to the North Shore, making the clubhouse an ideal venue for private parties for those who wanted to get away from the prying eyes of law enforcement during Prohibition (1920–1933). Lookouts could give ample warning to partiers to dispose of any evidence. A gambling casino and speakeasy was allegedly run at the clubhouse, with refreshments supplied by "Squint" Worthington. It is little wonder that the clubhouse was renamed the North Shore Tavern in 1927. The Arrowhead Lake Company sold the lake and tavern to the Los Angeles Turf Club in 1946. The Los Angeles Turf Club donated the tavern to the University of California, which ran a non-profitable conference center there. UCLA took over in 1982, reopening it in 1985 as a summer camp and retreat center called Bruin Woods; architect James Spencer, FAIA, was responsible for the design of the upgrade and enlargement of the facilities. (Both, RK.)

CLOUDLAND, 1920. Cloudland resort was conceived as a mega-resort consisting of three locations, the first of which was to be located approximately one mile west of the Arrowhead Springs Resort just below Marshall Peak on the Fred Brush Ranch. Australian architect William Harry Hillier designed Cloudland and envisioned the facilities would include a hotel, clubhouse, open-air theater, and convention center. Myron Carr, the promoter of the resort, wanted to sell 5,000 memberships for $1,000 each. The funds raised would then fund construction. Locals in San Bernardino were not enthusiastic about the project, but enough funds were raised by 1920 to acquire the property, construct a road, and complete some initial work at the site. In August 1921, Carr was involved in an automobile accident, and he died a month later. Carr's death effectively ended the Cloudland project. A 1924 fire destroyed the little that remained of Cloudland, including the original Fred Brush Ranch buildings. Today, only the road remains. The above rendering–from the front page of a *San Bernardino Daily Sun* article dated August 29, 1920–shows Hillier's architectural vision. (DW.)

Chief Sagital. Chief Sagital, a Native American man who lived near the Little Bear Lake Resort, dressed in full regalia to greet visitors. A *Los Angeles Times* article from 1922 states, "As soon as the snow is gone, construction will commence on the group of buildings that will form the little village of Sagital (which in Indian dialect means Arrowhead)." The Little Bear post office had the name "Sagital" before the area was known as Lake Arrowhead. (RK.)

The Village, June 24, 1922, to April 1979. Construction of the Village, designed by McNeal Swasey, began in 1921 and was completed by April 1922. The construction is shown here. Workers resided in the old Little Bear Lake Resort cabins that had been moved to nearby Cottage Grove. (RK.)

EARLY VIEWS OF THE VILLAGE. One of the distinctive features of the completed Village is the octagonal tower that acts as a focal point next to an archway that leads to the freestanding Dance Pavilion beyond it. Octagonal towers like these can be found in Normandy. It is used to visually anchor the center of the Village and lead people to the main attraction, the dance pavilion. (Both, RK.)

LAKE ARROWHEAD IN ARROWHEAD WOODS, CALIFORNIA

10412   DAILY SCENE IN THE VILLAGE   112961

DANCE PAVILION. One would not expect to find a polygonal building—much less a dodecagon (12 sides)—in a typical medieval village, yet it works both visually and pragmatically. Formerly called the Casino, the Dance Pavilion was later used as a cafeteria in the 1940s and as a penny arcade in the 1960s and 1970s. It now houses a restaurant and some shops. It was so exceptional a structure that it is the only one of the original buildings in the Village that was saved from destruction when the Village was used in a "Burn-to-Learn" exercise in April 1979. Unfortunately, today, the interior space that was once the grand dance hall is no longer visible because it has been divided for separate uses. The below photograph of the interior of the Dance Pavilion shows the space in all its glory. (Right, DW; below, UCLA-BP.)

DEMISE OF THE OLD VILLAGE, 1979. The Village remained the center of the Lake Arrowhead community until 1978, when a group of investors headed by George Coult and Jerry Jackson purchased both the Village and Lodge. Considering the Village a fire hazard that was too costly to renovate, they decided to start over. Jackson was a retired fireman who felt the "Burn-to-Learn" exercise would provide a great opportunity for the mountain's fire personnel. The Village was burned three or four times as practice. In April 1979, a monthlong "Burn-to-Learn" exercise was conducted with the Lake Arrowhead Fire Protection District, the San Bernardino County Fire Departments, and the Air Corps. All of the structures in the Village were burned in the exercise except the Dance Pavilion, post office, bank, and real estate office. (Both, ROWHS.)

THE NEW VILLAGE, 1981. Approximately two years after the infamous "Burn-to-Learn" exercise, the new Lake Arrowhead Village opened, looming 10 times larger than the original. It was designed by David Klages of Costa Mesa. Ownership has changed hands several times since 1981, and today, 40 years after the construction of the New Village, it is again in need of major repairs. (AL.)

ORCHARD BAY AUTO CAMP, 1922. The gatehouse originally served as the entrance for the Orchard Bay Auto Camp. For $1 per day, guests were provided with running water, toilets, firewood, cooking facilities, and tables. There was space for 1,000 cars. In 1928, the gatehouse was converted into a three-bedroom cottage. Orchard Bay was named after the apple trees that grew nearby. In the early 2000s, a new apple orchard was planted along the lakefront walking trail. (DW.)

CAMP FLEMING, 1922. Named after pioneer sawmill operator James Fleming, the lodge and 100-cottage Camp Fleming was commissioned by Ray S. Turner and designed by McNeal Swasey in 1922. By the late 1920s, the camp had capacity for 500 people and included a camp store and boat rentals. It operated until the early 1950s, when Turner retired. Nothing more remains of Camp Fleming; it has all been replaced by homes and condominiums. (JL.)

THE GRILL, 1922. The dictionary defines a ramada as "an open shelter, often having a dome-shaped roof, installed on beaches and picnic grounds." Camp Fleming boasted that its campers were provided space near a huge "Ramada" with the capacity to prepare food for as many as 500 people. The Ramada was better known as the Grill and was, at one point, run by the owners of the Village Inn. (CSL-FM.)

SKEET SHOOTING, 1920s. Boating and fishing were not the only sports popular during the 1920s. People participated in many outdoor sports, including swimming, archery, horseback riding, duck hunting, and skeet shooting. Both men and women took part in these activities. Here, some women are practicing their skills near where Papoose Lake is now located. (RK.)

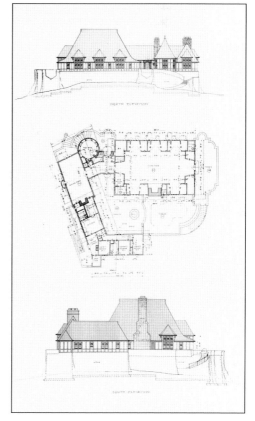

THE ISLAND HOUSE, 1922. This project was probably a clubhouse or hunting lodge designed for Lone Pine Island. Existing blueprints show servant's quarters and a gun room but no other bedrooms. Six small rooms, some with sinks, approximately five by eight feet, flank the living room. It was never built. McNeal Swasey and McAfee are listed as architects. A rendering appeared on the front page of the *Los Angeles Times* on February 26, 1922. (DW.)

THE VILLAGE INN, 1923. Designed by Swasey and McAfee, it is estimated that the 40-room Village Inn (with 60 additional rooms in adjacent cottages) cost $80,000 to build. The roof of the Inn is particularly interesting, with a thatched effect created by laying the shingles in irregular courses. It was managed by the Arlington and its sister resort, the Arlington Lodge, as a more economic choice. Unfortunately, wintertime occupancy lagged. Seeking to increase revenues, in 1924, the Inn was marketed as home to a "Mountain Lake Club." This venture was not successful and in 1925, the Village Inn was purchased by members of the film industry who changed its name to the Screen Club and turned it into a private club. In 1926, the Village Inn reopened under its old name. In 1938, a fire led to the temporary closing of the inn. It survived until April 1979, when it became the first of the Village buildings to succumb in the "Burn- to-Learn" exercise. (Above, JL; left, USC-AFAL.)

A Lake View of the Lodge
Lake Arrowhead, California

ARLINGTON LODGE, 1923. There were three main places to stay in Lake Arrowhead that were built in the 1920s. The Arlington Lodge, the Village Inn, and the most secluded—the North Shore Tavern. Opened in 1923, the Norman-style Arlington Lodge, located adjacent to the old Lake Arrowhead Village, was the most elegant of the three. Arlington Lodge, designed by McNeal Swasey, opened its doors to 1,000 affluent guests on June 23, 1923, with a midnight champagne party (despite Prohibition), the cuisine of a world-famous chef, and a dance. Guests also enjoyed the orchestra and toured the drawing rooms and the gracious bedchambers complete with private baths. Guests entered through an archway into a massive lobby with 45-foot ceilings and a huge fireplace. (Above, JL; right, DW.)

ARLINGTON LODGE

A-22   LAKE ARROWHEAD LODGE   SA-H1221

BEFORE AND AFTER THE FIRE. In the fall of 1938, tragedy struck when a fire, thought to have started in the kitchen, swept through the 150-room Arlington Lodge, destroying the east wing and lobby. It was quickly rebuilt and reopened in the spring of 1939 as the Arrowhead Lodge. The rebuilt lodge separated the public spaces and kitchen from the guest rooms. New construction was on the right, while the original portion of the lodge was on the left. The reimagined Arrowhead Lodge stayed in operation until 1973, when economics forced its closure. Three years later, the lodge was torn down. Its demise preceded the razing of the Village in 1979. In 1982, a year after the new Village opened, a new 176-room Arrowhead Hilton resort was built. (Both, JL.)

Lake Arrowhead Lodge

GOLF COURSE, 1924.
In addition to offering fishing, hiking, horseback riding, and boating, the Arrowhead Lake Company wanted to create a complete recreational experience for guests, including golf. In 1924, a nine-hole course was built with a small clubhouse that stood where the current maintenance building of the Lake Arrowhead Golf Club now stands. McNeal Swasey drew plans for a more extensive clubhouse, but that design never materialized. (Both, DW.)

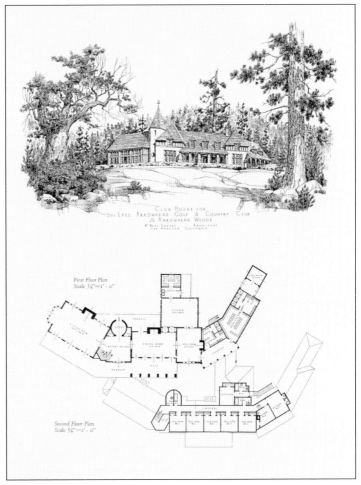

TYLER MILLS, 1870s. The golf course originally operated as a nine-hole course but fell into disuse for a number of years until the lake and properties were sold by the Los Angeles Turf Club to the Lake Arrowhead Development Company (LADC) in 1960. The above image shows Joseph B. Tyler's first mill, known as the Grass Valley Mill. The below image shows Tyler's second Grass Valley Sawmill. Both mills operated in the 1870s and were located on the site of the current golf course. The clear-cutting of trees in Grass Valley was originally intended to help create space for a lake bed intended to be part of a series of lakes that would be used for irrigation and supply water to the orange groves below. When that plan fell through, other uses of the valley were contemplated, and plans for the golf course eventually materialized. (Both, RK.)

ALPINE TERRACE RESORT, 1926. The Alpine Terrace Resort was originally built by Greg and Julia Dexter in Strawberry Flat, one of the first locations in the San Bernardino Mountains to have full-time residents. Strawberry Flat was so named because of the many wild strawberry fields in the area. The Dexter family also owned one of the sawmills and built many of the cabins in the area. When the Alpine Terrace Resort was built, it consisted of a dance pavilion and a number of small cabins for guests, including the first cabin built in Strawberry Flat, which dated to 1875. During the 1930s, it served as a frequent meeting place for the Worthwhile Club (originally the Diaper Club), a women's service club formed to help families in need. The corresponding men's club was called the Spit and Argue Club. The resort was sold in 1944. Several owners later, it reopened as Antler's Inn in 1968. In 1988, it was designated a state historical landmark. Today, it continues to offer lodging, and its restaurant is well known on the mountain for its fine dining. (RK.)

CLUB ARROWHEAD, 1928. Developed by the Atkins Company as an upscale real estate development, Club Arrowhead (of the Pines) flourished during the 1920s. Rumor has it that Bugsy Siegel ran a gambling, bootlegging, and prostitution ring at the club during Prohibition, although that is highly unlikely, as he did not move to California until after Prohibition ended. There is evidence that these activities did occur, however. John Adam's locally brewed apple brandy and Squint Worthington's "White Mule" whiskey were served. Patrons were warned of eminent raids through the use of mirror signals on the road up the mountain to a sheriff's station informer. Children, too, were employed as lookouts and were rewarded with treats. The club's amenities included an Olympic-sized swimming pool, a ski run, tennis courts, and riding stables. It is now a venue for the arts called the Tudor House. (Both, RK.)

INTERIOR OF CLUB ARROWHEAD

1405

Four

THE MYTHMAKERS
HOUSES OF THE GOLDEN AGE

A NEW ARCHITECTURAL STYLE. The following caption from an article in *Architectural Record* (1923) describes the new architectural style in Arrowhead: "In determining the style of architecture, Mr. Swasey, after studying the landscape . . . turned to the early English and Norman type of village for inspiration. The steep roofs, which were one of the first considerations, have the twofold purpose of adapting themselves to the mountain slopes and recalling the peaked pine trees, as also the more practical one of shedding the snow." (JL.)

LITTLE BEAR LODGE, 1922. This house, described on the permit as "an English Cottage on Lots 10 & 11" cost $25,000 to build—a substantial sum in 1922. It is most likely the first of the great houses built on the lake and was commissioned by J.B. Van Nuys, one of the developers of the lake. It was designed by McNeal Swasey with H.C. McAfee, Associate. Later additions included work by Morgan, Walls and Clements and E. Charles and Louise Parke. Little Bear Lodge was included in the December 1922 issue of the *Architectural Record* and is one of the few Arrowhead buildings to be featured in a national publication. Notice how the half timbering is featured on both the exterior and interior of the house. (Above, JL; below, USC-AFAL.)

MILTON GETZ HOUSE, AKA "MINKOT," 1923. Designed by McNeal Swasey for banker Milton E. Getz at a cost of $12,500, this house was later owned by movie star Dan Duryea. The IMDB biography on Duryea states that he was best known for his role as a "sniveling, deliberately taunting" villain in Westerns. Duryea wanted a lakefront house. His wife, on the other hand, wanted a mink coat. To satisfy his desire for a house and his wife's hankering, he purchased the house and named it "Minkot." (JL.)

PRINCE MASSINOFF HOUSE, 1923. Alexis Massinoff, a self-described Russian prince, had Chas. E. Bugg build this stone house for him and his two sisters to replicate his manor house in Russia. Putty Henck described the prince as "quite a talker and very opinionated" and stated the family lived in the house until the early 1980s. It has an asymmetric main gable and is one of the few stone structures in Arrowhead. (DW.)

MAMIE MODINI-WOOD HOUSE, 1924. This early lakefront house was designed by McNeal Swasey and published in the 1925 issue of *Pacific Coast Architect* as an example of Lake Arrowhead's Norman architecture; the photographs shown here are from that publication. The elevation is very similar to a farmhouse (sans the bay window) in Ralph Adam Cram's 1917 book *Farm Houses Manor Houses Minor Châteaux Small Churches in Normandy and Brittany*. Most architects at this time would have been familiar with Cram's books, so this is not a surprise. Although the house is sometimes referred to as the Shirley Temple House, Temple never owned it. However, she was a guest of the "Canary of the Pacific," opera singer Mamie Modini-Wood. The house has been restored and still looks much as it does in these images. (Above, CSL-FM; below, USC-AFAL.)

RINDGE/ADAMSON LODGE, 1924. This house was originally built by Ralph B. Wilson in 1924 from designs by R.M. Finlayson, a Palm Springs architect, at a cost of $20,000. In 1928, May Rindge and her daughter, Rhoda Adamson, purchased the property and hired McNeal Swasey to make "alterations and addition to present residence and garage and a new laundry building" for $20,000. Since the Adamson family were owners of the Malibu Tile Company, it seemed possible that the remodel included elaborate tilework but there is no indication that this was ever the case. A *Los Angeles Times* newspaper article from 2013 claims that celebrity architect Paul Revere Williams, FAIA, worked on the house at some point when actor Lon Chaney is said to have owned the property. (Both, MAHF.)

P.G. Winnett House, 1924. This house was built for P.G. Winnett, one of the founders of Bullocks Wilshire. D.P. Collins signed the building permit. It cost $12,000 to build—a substantial sum in 1924. Bullocks was founded in 1907 by John G. Bullock with the support of the Broadway Department Store owner Arthur Letts. In 1923, Bullock and Winnett bought out Letts's interest, and the companies were separated. In 1929, Bullock and Winnett opened a luxury branch they named Bullocks Wilshire. After Bullock's death in 1933, Winnett took over and was personally responsible for the development of its flagship store, Bullock's Wilshire. Winnett was known for personally visiting each of the stores every week, shaking hands with customers, and handing out chocolate kisses. The house immediately adjacent was designed as the servant's quarters, complete with a beautiful stone terrace overlooking the lake. (Above, DW; below, SS.)

C.F. Fellows House, 1924. Designed by Glenn Elwood Smith, AIA, a University of Southern California architectural graduate, this early home was built for nationally known railroad man C.F. Fellows. Smith worked with Myron Hunt and designed a number of significant local structures in the Pasadena area, including Pasadena's Art Deco Masonic lodge. (DW.)

Jahns / Curtis M. Willock Main House, 1926. The house on the lot immediately to the east of the Willock chauffeur's quarters was originally designed at a cost of $8,000 for Mr. & Mrs. W.H. Jahns, an automotive piston manufacturer and his wife. Curtis M. Willock, known as the designer of the world's first electric golf cart, purchased the Jahns' house and pulled two additional permits for alterations, using San Francisco architect Thomas B. Mulvin for the alterations to the house. This image is from an early publication on Lake Arrowhead. (DW.)

PHILENA W. HUBBARD HOUSE, 1927. This house was commissioned by Philena W. Hubbard, who was said to be one of the wealthiest women in Redlands after inheriting the estate of her father, Clarence J. Wetmore. Wetmore was a pioneer California vineyardist and founder of the Cresta Blanca Winery, located near Livermore, and a member of the first graduating class of the University of California in 1873. Hubbard hired E. Charles and Louise A. Parke to design her home, which cost $15,671–quite a substantial sum in 1927. E. Charles Parke worked as a specification writer for Albert C. Martin Sr. and was a chief draftsman for McNeal Swasey before going into practice on his own. His wife, Louise A. Parke, is often listed on building permits alongside him, although it is not clear what her role was. (DW.)

FRANK L. FOX HOUSE, 1929. This north shore house was designed by architect Alfred F. Priest. The permit was approved on June 29, 1929, exactly four months prior to the stock market crash that occurred on October 29, 1929. The permit estimated the cost of construction at $15,000, but a former owner said he believed it actually cost $10,500 to build. This is not surprising, given the economic situation of the time. It is said that Aline Barnsdale (of Hollyhock House and Barnsdale Park fame) owned the property at one point. (BC.)

ROD LA ROCQUE HOUSE, 1929.
Shortly after Rod La Rocque married actor Vilma Bansky in 1927, he hired architect Frances J. Catton to design a house for them in Lake Arrowhead. Catton was the architect for the Los Angeles Board of Education and designed the Beverly Vista School Administration Building in Beverly Hills before venturing out on his own. The La Rocque house is located next door to the Sidney Franklin House that was built in 1935. Noted architect Cliff May later owned the house after selling his smaller Arrowhead house, the Willock chauffeur's quarters located several houses to the east, to noted architectural photographer Maynard Parker. Rod and his new bride, Vilma, are pictured at left holding a day's catch. (Above, DW; right, UCLA-BP.)

CURTIS M. WILLOCK CHAUFFEUR'S HOUSE, 1932. This small lakefront house was initially designed as a garage and chauffeur's living quarters by Stiles O. Clements at a cost of $1,000. Famous Southern California architect Cliff May, credited with the development of the California ranch house, owned this house for a while and had noted Southern California landscape architect Thomas "Tommy" Dolliver Church design a large terrace for him, as shown in these before and after photographs. May sold the property to famed architectural photographer Maynard Parker, whose family lived there for many years. The house has been extensively remodeled, and Church's terraces were replaced by a new house. (Above, AD&A; left, DC.)

Five

THE MYTHMAKERS
THE GOLDEN AGE CONTINUES

"North Shore Tavern"
LAKE ARROWHEAD

POST CARD

MAY
3 PM
1930

Mrs. G. H. Hazelwood
1769 - Neale St
San Diego
Calif.

Dear Mother;
when we woke up this
morning it was snowing its
the first time In I ever seen it
come down, it sure is cold
but it's a darling place we are
staying steam heat & everything
Having a grand time
Love — Franna

LIFE CONTINUES. Because of the movie industry, Arrowhead weathered the Great Depression relatively unscathed, with construction continuing at both large and small scales. The area's recreational pursuits also thrived, as shown on this 1930 postcard. The area's most expensive home was built at this time, the Château des Fleurs, as well as its most famous, Rudolf Schindler's groundbreaking design for the world's first Modern A-frame. Others saved time and money with mail-order Sears catalog houses. (JL.)

63

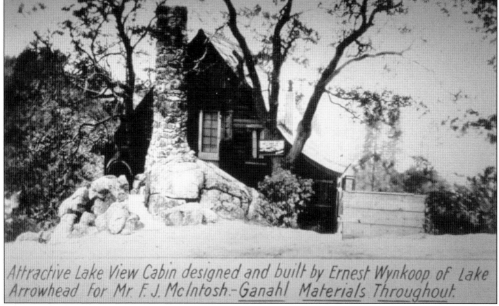

Attractive Lake View Cabin designed and built by Ernest Wynkoop of Lake Arrowhead for Mr. F.J. McIntosh.-Ganahl Materials Throughout.

BOULDER CREST, 1930. WPA engineer Ernest Wynkoop designed this cabin for F.J. McIntosh. Wynkoop was involved in a number of projects on the mountain, including the modernist design of a post office for Blue Jay. Boulder Crest was designed in a vernacular style more like the turn-of-the-century romantic Victorian cabins rather than the high-style Anglo-French Norman designs popular at the time. (JL.)

SHIRLEY TEMPLE HUNTING LODGE, 1931. There are two homes associated with the name Shirley Temple on the mountain—a hunting lodge and a lakefront house. Temple did spend a great deal of time in Arrowhead but never actually owned any property on the mountain. This is a photograph of the hunting lodge that was built and owned by producer/director Delmer Daves in 1931. Temple was a frequent visitor at the lodge, as were Clark Gable and Jimmy Stewart. (DW.)

CHÂTEAU DES FLEURS, 1931. Designed for Katharine Iten, the Saltine cracker heiress, this house cost over $100,000 to build. It was rumored that the house was brought from France stone by stone, but this is not true—only elements such as the front door surround made that journey. It was designed by William Lee Woollett Sr., AIA, and his son, William Lee Woollett Jr., FAIA, both prominent Los Angeles architects. The driveway concrete patterning is said to have been designed to look like Saltine crackers. The custom tile ceiling in the dining room is based on the scenes found in the Bayeux Tapestry thought to date from the 11th century and considered "one of the supreme achievements of the Norman Romanesque." The Woolletts come from a long line of artists and architects. Woollett Jr. received his fellowship in the American Institute of Architects for his etchings of important WPA projects. A beautiful mural graces the ceiling of a living room niche. There is also a pipe organ in the house. (DW.)

SHADY POINT, 1931. Located on the north shore of Lake Arrowhead, this home was designed for attorney John O'Melveny, one of the investors in the Arrowhead Lake Company, by Roland Coate Sr., FAIA. The north shore was home to many celebrities in the 1920s, which led to it getting the nickname the "Beverly Hills of the mountains." The irregularly shaped and asymmetrical house is largely unchanged on the exterior, which is clad with stucco and wood shingles under a steeply pitched hip roof punctuated by dormers. The visible rafter tails slightly flare the shingles at the roof edges, creating a skirting effect typical of the French Revival style. Most of the large trees once found on the property, which gave it the name Shady Point, have been killed by insects in recent years. Shady Point was individually listed in the National Register of Historic Places in 2009. A carved squirrel adorns the stair handrail. (Both, DW.)

GEORGE O. NOBLE HOUSE, 1931. Noble, a wealthy Pasadena mining engineer, is listed on the permit as the original owner/architect/builder. His Pasadena home (Viola's house in the 2005 movie *Monster-in-Law*) was designed by master architect Wallace Neff, FAIA, in 1927. Neff designed many beautiful French Norman houses, so it is a bit puzzling why he was not the architect on this project. Perhaps he had some input on the design. Photographer Walter Sanders photographed the house in 1945. Many charming details can still be found throughout the house. Regardless of whether Neff was involved in the design, someone did pay careful attention to details, as shown in this tile insert by the front door of the house. (Both, DW.)

"VANITY FAIR," 1932. This cabin was designed by architect Van Evera Bailey for famed silent-film director Chester M. Franklin. Bailey apprenticed with Prairie School architect William Gray Purcell in Portland, Oregon. After moving to Southern California, Bailey worked with Richard Neutra. In 1933, Bailey and Purcell designed the Cubist Modern Purcell house in Palm Springs. Many of Bailey's Southern California houses evoke a Streamline Moderne aesthetic. Bailey also appears to have designed a home for himself in the Emerald Bay area, but the current house on the lot was built many years later and most likely not by Bailey. He returned to Portland in 1936. (DV.)

HAPPY LANDING, 1933. Roland Coate Sr., architect of John O'Melvany's Shady Point, also designed Leigh M. Battson & Lucy Doheny's home. It is located on the largest parcel of privately owned land on the lake. There are several houses on the property, with the most visible being the lakefront boathouse. Coate had once been a partner with architect Gordon Kaufman, FAIA, where he worked on the design of Los Angeles's St. Paul's Episcopal Cathedral and All Saints Episcopal Church in Pasadena. This estate was published in *Architectural Digest* in 1938, as shown in these photographs from that issue. Battson was the director of Union Oil Company of California and married "Ned" Doheny's widow Lucy Smith Doheny. Lucy Estelle Doheny was the daughter of Edward "Ned" Doheny Jr. and Lucy Battson, granddaughter of Edward L. Doheny. (Both, AD&A.)

PINE SHELTER, 1933. This house for Dr. Hill Hastings, a prominent Los Angeles surgeon, was designed at the beginning of the 1930s by Stiles O. Clements, AIA, head of the Arrowhead Lake Architectural Committee. Dr. Hastings was the son of Thomas Horace Hastings, a relative of industrialist Henry Flagler, founder of Miami and Palm Beach, Florida. The town of Hastings, Florida, was named after Thomas Hastings, who ran an experimental vegetable farm to raise crops for the Flagler hotels. This lakefront house is interesting in that it does not have the half timbering so typical of many of McNeal Swasey's more French Norman designs, but it does exude a rustic cottage feel with its clipped roofs. This feature can be seen in many Arrowhead cabins built around time. The house was published in *Architectural Digest* in 1938. A 1934 *Los Angeles Times* article refers to the house as Pine Shelter. (Both, USC-AFAL.)

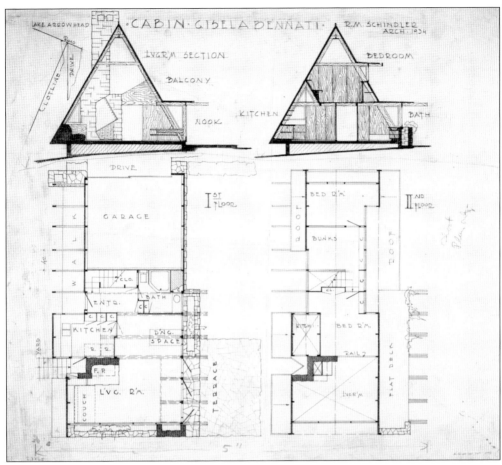

GISELA BENNATI CABIN, 1934. Rudolf Schindler designed several other "triangle houses," but this was the first to be realized. Heralded as the world's first modern A-frame house, it is now popular worldwide. The Arrowhead Woods Architectural Committee at the time stipulated that all new construction be of French/English Norman design. Architectural historian Esther McCoy stated that the reason the design was approved was that none of the members of the architectural committee had ever been to Europe, and Schindler convinced the committee to approve the design by showing them photographs of steep-roofed French Norman buildings. This is a wonderful story, but alas, it is probably not completely true. Architectural committee chair Stiles O. Clements had lived in France while studying at the École des Beaux-Arts in Paris, and even if he had not been present at Schindler's presentation, he certainly would have known about the design. (Both, AD&A.)

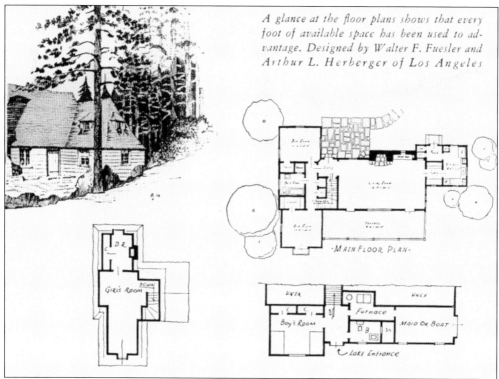

A glance at the floor plans shows that every foot of available space has been used to advantage. Designed by Walter F. Fuesler and Arthur L. Herberger of Los Angeles

"MONTCROFT," 1934. Fuesler and Herberger designed this house, located one lot west of Willock's chauffeur's quarters, for Vincent Montgomery in 1934. Willock also owned the lot to the east. Permits list the cost of construction as $6,000. In 1936, Montgomery hired Howard E. Jones to design a garage. Jones has been called the busiest architect in San Bernardino between World War I and World War II. Two-time Olympic swimmer and actor Buster Crabbe later owned the house at some point. (AL.)

SIDNEY FRANKLIN HOUSE, 1935. Permits show that film director and producer Sidney Franklin had Pasadena architects Marston and Mayberry design this house. Cary Grant and Barbara Hutton were married at Frank Vincent's house in 1942, which has been said is this house. A 1940 building permit, however, puts Vincent's property several lots to the east. Perhaps Vincent purchased Franklin's home at some point? In any case, photographs exist showing Grant and Hutton at the house. (DW.)

HILLTOP, 1935. Kate Van Nuys Page, sister of J.B. Van Nuys, had this house designed for her by Robert Farquhar, FAIA. Farquhar, an MIT graduate, also attended the École de Beaux-Arts and worked for Hunt & Hunt and Carrérre and Hastings before opening his own office in Los Angeles. Page planted the many daffodils, which still grace the property, to remind her of the San Fernando Valley daffodil fields of her youth. The house was later owned by MCA founder Jules Stein and then J. Watson Webb Jr., a Vanderbilt heir. Webb nicknamed the property "Hilltop" after one of the Vanderbilt mansions. Numerous Hollywood celebrities stayed at the property. USC-trained architect Grahm Latta, AIA, designed a cottage which Marilyn Monroe affectionately called her Happy Hut. The most recent owner added a large solarium and other amenities. (Both, DW.)

LEWIS STONE HOUSE, 1937. This house was built for Academy Award–winning actor Lewis Stone in 1937. Stone received his Oscar for Best Actor for his role in the 1929 movie *The Patriot*. The house cost $12,000 to build and was designed by Edward P. Finnegan at a cost of $12,000. The most striking feature of this house is its imposing roof. Architect John Lyles, AIA, did an addition to the rear of the house enclosing the former back porch and gently raising the roof to add a bit of height to the family room that opens to the rear yard. Finnegan received his B.S. in Architecture from the University of Pennsylvania and his architectural license in 1924. These photographs offer before and after views of the rear of the house. (Left, DW; below, JL.)

THE WHITE HOUSE, 1939. Ted R. Cooper built this house for himself along Highway 173. It is unusual in that it is one of the few houses that started construction at the beginning of World War II. Perhaps because it was not a lakefront home, the Coopers decided to build another very similar house for themselves on the north shore close to the North Shore Tavern. (MSS.)

WINDSWEPT, 1944. This house was also built by Ted R. Cooper and is still owned by the family. It has many features similar to those of the White House, including a circular entry tower with a custom weathervane sporting the name of the house. The interiors were designed by Gustave Plochere, known for the Plochere Color System, one of the first commercially available color systems in the United States. Max Factor Studios, paint companies Dunn-Edwards, Benjamin Moore and Ameritone, all referenced the Plochere Color System, as did Disney, the National Broadcasting Company (NBC) and various universities such as Stanford, MIT, and the University of California. Much of Plochere's original design is still intact in this house. Windswept graced the cover of the Los Angeles Times HOME Magazine in 1948. (MSS.)

THE COMPOUND, 1946. This house was designed by noted Long Beach architect K.S. Wing, FAIA, for H.B. Nicholson, a renowned Aztec scholar. Started in 1937, the project was not completed until after World War II ended. After Nicholson's passing, it was purchased in 1959 and has remained in the family of the second owner ever since. The clean lines of the structure and careful attention to detail give the project an aura of elegance and sophistication, as displayed in these entry gates. The classic movie *Magnificent Obsession* (1954), staring Rock Hudson and Jane Wyman, was filmed here. Wyman was married to Ronald Reagan at the time. Reagan's familiarity with the area was certainly advantageous when, after the large San Fernando earthquake in 1971, there was discussion about lowering the lake by 70 feet. Reagan was governor of California at the time and would have undoubtedly understood the negative impact of such an action. (Above, LBD; left, DW.)

Six

THE ESCAPISTS
RESPITE FROM THE GREAT DEPRESSION

MOVIES AND MORE. People needed an escape from their worries during the Depression, and movies provided much-needed relief. Since so many movies were shot at Lake Arrowhead, the area fared better than most. Recreation on the mountain flourished during the 1930s, as did retreats for people looking for spiritual enlightenment. This is a photograph of Chick Merrick with his record-breaking 37-inch, 16-pound, 9-ounce trout caught in Lake Arrowhead in 1933. (DW.)

TOTEM POLE POINT, 1931. The totem poles shown here were originally erected for the filming of the 1931 Warner Brothers movie *River's End*. *River's End* was not the only movie filmed at the site, as in 1936, MGM filmed *Rose Marie* there. The totem poles remained for many years until the Moreland Development Company subdivided the site and sold 19 lakefront lots. Large lakefront luxury houses have replaced the totem poles; by the time they were removed, they had sadly deteriorated beyond salvage. (RK.)

WILLOW WOODS, 1932. Originally a logging camp in the 1800s, this site operated as a campground in the 1920s. In 1932, several small cabins and a restaurant were added. In 1984, the current owners purchased it and renamed it Willow Woods. It operates as a collection of artisan shops and restaurants and a wedding venue. It was once owned by Frank Adams, who was part of an artistic community called the Skyforesters. (DW).

THE LAKE ARROWHEAD YACHT CLUB, 1932. Originally loosely organized to race motorboats in 1930, the Lake Arrowhead Yacht Club incorporated in 1932 to include both motorboat racing and sailing. From 1948 to 1951, the club was located in the North Shore Tavern. Prior to that, the club's facility was first in a storefront in the Village and then located in the Arlington Lodge, where club members utilized the lodge's food concession. In 1954, a clubhouse was built on the south shore on land purchased by the club in 1945. This small clubhouse was expanded in 1960 to include a bar, a kitchen, and restrooms. In 1979, the clubhouse building was again expanded to its current configuration. The below photograph shows the Olympic class of Star sailboats that raced on the lake from 1940 to 1961. The water ski and motorboat races sponsored by the Lake Arrowhead Yacht Club were discontinued in 1969. (Both, DW.)

SKIING ON THE MOUNTAIN. The first recorded account of skiing in Southern California is in pioneer logger Joseph B. Tyler's diary entry dated 1873. In 1921, ski pioneer Eddie Juan arrived in Arrowhead from Switzerland. He was one of the first skilled skiers in Southern California. A sling lift was located behind the Lake Arrowhead village school, where the fire station currently is, as was a 1931 ski jump. (KSL.)

SNOW VALLEY, 1939. In 1937, ski jump champion Sverre Engen bought the food concession building at Fish Camp and changed its name to Snow Valley. Noted Southern California architect Wallace Neff designed the new facilities, but they burned down in 1949. In 1953, a new, larger lodge was built and is still in use. It is Southern California's oldest ski resort and home to its first steel-towered single chair lift. (HL.)

Camp Mozumdar, 1936. Akbay Kumar "A.K." Mozumdar was a popular spiritual leader and writer often associated with the New Thought Movement in the United States. He was born in Calcutta, India, and immigrated to the United States in 1904. One of his followers, San Diego architect William P. Lodge, AIA, designed this temple for him for people of all religious faiths to worship together. Some have said the design was modeled after the Taj Mahal, although Lodge denies this. It is built of poured concrete and stone rumored to be designed as a bomb shelter. (JL.)

MAZUMDOR TEMPLE, CEDARPINES PARK, CALIF.   ROSECRAFT

Mozumdar Temple Interior. Mozumdar died before the temple was completed, and the interior with murals depicting the life of Christ (shown in the rendering below) was never realized. After Mozumdar's death, the YMCA purchased the property but sold it in the 1970s to Rev. Sun Myung Moon's Unification Church. (M.)

BLUE JAY Ice Skating Rink I-I/2 Mi. West Of Lake Arrowhead.

BLUE JAY ICE SKATING RINK, 1939. Blue Jay got its start with the lumber industry, as the Caley Mill was located near the center of town. In 1867, a group of Native Americans burned Frank Talmadge's sawmill there. In the 1920s, Blue Jay became a year-round recreation area. When Blue Jay Bay would freeze over in the winter, ice skating became popular. A year-round rink was built in 1939. Ice Follies star Carol Probst and her husband, Walter, brought Olympic-caliber skating to Blue Jay by building the Ice Castle in 1983. Unfortunately, a heavy snow in 2001 caused the roof of public skating rink to collapse, ending the era of public skating in Blue Jay. A 22,000-square-foot office building designed by Robert Kite, AIA, now occupies the site of the former public skating rink. (Both, RK.)

MOVIE POINT, 1927. Numerous movies have been filmed in Lake Arrowhead. What is now Point Hamiltair was once called Movie Point because of the village that was built for the filming of *Sunrise* (1927), the first movie to be nominated for an Oscar in four categories and the first to win in three. *Of Human Hearts* (1938) was also filmed at the site, as was *The Yearling* (1947), starring Gregory Peck and Jane Wyman. Arrowhead local June Lockhart had a role in the movie. *The Yearling* was supposed to take place in Florida, and since palm trees did not grow in Arrowhead, the studios brought potted palm trees for use in the film, as seen in the photograph below. The palm trees were brought back down the mountain once the filming was complete. (Right, ROWHS; below, RK.)

ARROWHEAD SPRINGS HOTEL, 1939. The current hotel is the fourth one built at the hot springs. Before the hotels, Indigenous peoples used the healing hot springs beneath the arrowhead on Arrowhead Mountain for thousands of years. The current structure was designed by architects Gordon B. Kaufman, FAIA (known for his work on the Hoover Dam), and Paul Williams, FAIA (AIA Gold Medalist and first African American member of the AIA). Dorothy Draper designed the interiors. Draper was the founder of the first interior design firm in the United States. The hotel was Hollywood's A-list favorite. During World War II, the hotel was turned into a Navy hospital and served over 6,000 servicemen. It reverted to a hotel after the war until it was sold to Campus Crusade for Christ as their world headquarters. It has since been sold to the San Manual Band of Mission Indians. (Both, RT.)

Seven

FLYING HIGH
THE AVIATORS OF LAKE ARROWHEAD

AVIATORS HAVING FUN. Over the years, a number of aviators have called Lake Arrowhead home. Thomas Hamilton, John Northrop, "Jack" Lockheed, and Jack Maddux all had one or more homes in Arrowhead. This image shows Amelia Earhart being pulled on an aquaplane during a visit to Lake Arrowhead. Even Pancho Barnes had a connection to the community. The Arrowhead airfield located on the site of Squint Worthington's old ranch was once owned by Allen Paulson, the founder of Gulfstream Jets. (RK.)

FERNROCK RANCH, 1912. Caroline Dobbins originally had a large cabin at the Squirrel Inn. When the Rim of the World Highway was built, the cabin was demolished, and Dobbins built another large cabin nearby on what would later be called Fernwood Ranch. Her daughter Florence Mae married Thad Lowe Jr., son of the scientist/inventor Thaddeus S.C. Lowe Sr., who is sometimes considered the "father of the US Air Force." Lowe Sr.'s hot-air balloons were recruited for use in military aerial reconnaissance during the Civil War. Thad Jr. and Florence Mae had two children. Their daughter Florence "Pancho" Barnes was taught hunting and horseback riding by her grandfather Thaddeus Lowe Sr.—skills she probably practiced at Fernrock Ranch. (Both, SBCL.)

Hi-Lowe Farm, 1939. After Florence Dobbins Lowe died, Thaddeus Lowe Jr. built his own cabin nearby with his new wife, Ruth Ruel. His and Florence's daughter, Pancho, well known by this point as a stunt and test pilot trainer who once broke Amelia Earhart's speed record, was "grown and flown." Pancho's life was portrayed in the 1983 movie *The Right Stuff* and the 2009 PBS special *The Legend of Pancho Barnes and the Happy Bottom Riding Club.* The Lowe family lost much of its fortune during the Great Depression, and Thaddeus Lowe Jr. and Ruth came to live full-time at the Hi-Lowe Farm, which still stands. However, Fernrock Ranch has been replaced by Fernrock Estates, a condominium development built in 1970. (BP.)

HAMILTON NORTH SHORE HOUSE, 1928. George R. Brug built this house in 1928 for a cost of $10,000. It was designed by E. Charles Parke, a former draftsman for McNeal Swasey. Ethel Hamilton, wife of aviator Thomas Hamilton, known for the manufacture of the variable pitch propeller, later purchased the house. Shortly thereafter, her husband, Thomas Hamilton, negotiated and eventually acquired the entire peninsula directly across the lake on which he built several houses for his family and guests while maintaining the North Shore house as he and his wife's personal residence. In 1961, he subdivided part of his property on the peninsula and developed it into the subdivision he called Hamiltair, an eponym derived from his company's name "Hamilton Air." He sold the end of the Peninsula later. The tip of the peninsula is now the gated community of Point Hamiltair. The Records show that another permit was pulled in 1941 by a F.W. Smith and designed by F. Lea McPike after the Hamilton's sold the house. (Both, DW).

THE BOATHOUSE, 1937. Pioneering aviator Thomas Hamilton built the first structure on the peninsula, which was designed by celebrity architect Paul Revere Williams, FAIA. The Boathouse was said to be modeled after an old boathouse on the Thames River in England. It was originally designed as a party house with the first floor serving as a "float deck" where boats docked, the second floor offering a pavilion deck for parties, and the third floor having two small rooms for sail storage and a bathroom. Tom Selleck is said to have stayed there. Architect McDonald Beckett, nephew of architect Welton Beckett, purchased the property from Hamilton in the 1950s. Beckett owned the property for a number of years before selling it to the Davis family, who hired architect H.B. Leydenfrost to do an extensive remodel and addition in 1980. The current owners have attempted to restore the house to be closer to Williams's vision of the project as shown in this photograph. (JS.)

THE SISTERS' HOUSE, 1937. Thomas Hamilton's original house on the peninsula was said to be originally designed for his two daughters. The house and all the structures were designed by Paul Revere Williams, FAIA. Over the years, the house became known as the Sisters' House. Williams designed this English Country–style home using redwood, pine, and stucco, giving it a natural quality but not an overly rustic feel. It is said that Hamilton wanted his daughters to have experience learning the "fundamentals of housekeeping" and had them assist in the design of the interiors and furnishings. Sometime in the 1970s, the house was moved from its original location near the entrance of Hamiltair to its current lakefront location near the Boathouse. The house has been beautifully restored to its original condition. One of the upstairs bedrooms has a built-in bed and beautiful stenciling on the wood. (MF.)

THE GATEHOUSE, 1939. Also designed by Paul Williams, this house was originally located near the entrance to Thomas Hamilton's property and was the original guest house for the estate. Because of the proximity to the gate, it was named the Gatehouse. The Gatehouse, like the Sisters' House, had a thatched roof. Since Hamilton was unable to obtain fire insurance for the Gatehouse because of the thatching, he procured his own fire truck, which he housed in an adjacent building. Both structures have long since had their thatched roofs replaced with slate. When an actual gatehouse was built for Hamiltair, the original guest house was moved one block down the street. It was expanded at that time. When prospective buyers used to come to Hamiltair when it first opened, they would spend the night at the guest house. Hamilton stipulated that all interior lots would have to be sold first before he allowed any of the lakefront properties to be sold. (DW.)

THE STABLES, 1937 AND 1940. The stables were immediately adjacent to the original guest house. They were built in two phases, starting in 1937, with an expansion in 1940. Many years after the stables were no longer used, the stalls were converted into small apartments, and the building was eventually sold and converted into a house. This is the first structure one sees when entering Hamiltair. It never had a thatched roof. It is said that the stables were incorrectly built—during construction, the plans were accidentally reversed, and the main facade that faces south was actually meant to face the lake to the north. Adjacent to the stables are what had been the servants' quarters and fire house, which have been converted into condos. A large main house was designed for the Hamilton property but was never built. Paul Williams was the architect for all of Hamilton's buildings in Arrowhead. (Both, DW.)

JOHN NORTHROP HOUSES, 1946. John "Jack" Northrop built two houses in Arrowhead designed by Pasadena architect Garret Van Pelt, FAIA—one for $20,000 and another for $17,500 on the adjacent property. One of the cabins was known as the Northrop Aircraft Corporation cabin (above). Northrop had a long history in Lake Arrowhead. In 1924, he built the first "sling lift" in the mountains at Fish Camp (now known as Snow Valley). Before this lift was built, skiers had to hike up the hill with their equipment, often weighing nearly 20 pounds, to be able to ski down; if they were lucky, they could use a cumbersome rope tow. Northrop also is said to have designed an experimental boat. These photographs are from the Huntington Library Collection, filed under Northrop Aircraft Corporation cabin, Lake Arrowhead. (Both, HM.)

LOCKHEED CABIN, 1948. John Lockheed, son of Lockheed Aircraft Corporation founder Alan Lockheed, had a small cabin designed and built for him in Lake Arrowhead. It was designed by Burbank architect Lucille Bryant Raport, AIA, who was one of just 350 licensed female architects in the country at the time. Raport made her name designing mid-century houses and apartment buildings in the San Fernando Valley during its 1950s building boom. Julius Shulman photographed the cabin, and it was published in a 1948 *Los Angeles Times* article on modern mountain cabins. Rudolph Schindler's Lake Arrowhead Bennati cabin was also featured in the article. Raport received her architectural degree from the University of Kansas. After moving to Southern California, she was made junior partner at the firm of Harry Inge Johnston and was one of Skidmore, Owens, and Merrill's chief designers. She also studied with renowned architect Richard Neutra before establishing her own firm. (GRI.)

Eight

THE MODERNISTS
DAWNING OF A NEW AGE

ADVERTISING THE FUN. The period after the Lake Arrowhead Development Company purchased the lake in 1960 brought about many changes, and many new tracts were opened for development. The golf club was expanded, and many recreational opportunities were advertised, as shown in this *Los Angeles Times* advertisement. Even the architecture promoted here reflected this change, with many new and modern designs developed unlike anything else that had been seen on the mountain. (ROWHS.)

Grand Opening

Lake Arrowhead's Exclusive

North Shore

New magnificent view sites from $5990 frontages to 100 x 140 feet

First time offered & from $590 down

They're new, magnificent, and open! And only 90 minutes from Los Angeles in a story book setting on the most desirable end of the largest, most beautiful, finest privately owned lake in the southland. It's a giant lake with a 14 mile shoreline of hidden coves, beaches and 780 acres of blue water for sailing, water skiing, swimming and fishing yet private marinas and beaches are within a few minutes of your homesite. You can ride or hike amid aromatic pine forests, play tennis, golf on the 18 hole PGA course or just

chew sweet meadow grass and inhale great gulps of mountain air. A master planned lake community...what a place for the kids...for the family...for weekend or year round 4 season living...now or in the future. There's no other place like it and there's not much of it though because the sites are surrounded by permanent U.S. National Forests.

Complete modern shopping center. Water, power, gas, sewer and paved roads included in purchase price.

actual photos

Sold only by
Lake Arrowhead Development Company
Owners and developers
Excellent financing
Office at Village gate

– – – – SEND FOR FREE BROCHURE TODAY – – – –
LAKE ARROWHEAD DEVELOPMENT COMPANY
8348 Beverly Blvd., Los Angeles, California 90048
Call Collect (213) OL 1-2210 (Los Angeles)

Gentlemen. Send me free color brochure and full information by mail. No salesmen will visit except at request

Name
Address   Phone
City   State   Zip

95

LAKE ARROWHEAD COUNTRY CLUB, 1961. After falling into disuse after many years and returned to the cows, the original 9-hole golf course was expanded to 18 holes after Jules Berman and the Lake Arrowhead Development Company purchased the lake. In 1963, the back nine holes were carved out of the surrounding mountain, and a new clubhouse was commissioned to be designed by Richard L. Dorman, FAIA. It was a dramatic mid-century modern A-frame, which some called the largest A-frame in the world at the time of its construction. Honored guests at the opening of the clubhouse included Bob Hope, Bing Crosby, Dean Martin, and Tony Bennett. The project was published in the October 1961 issue of *Arts and Architecture*. (Above, A&A; below, DW.)

LAKE ARROWHEAD COUNTRY CLUB SHORTLY AFTER COMPLETION, 1964. Richard Dorman's work unifies landscape, exterior, and interior design in what was termed "total design." Dorman was also interested in trains, having written 13 books on narrow-gauge railroads. He built a 750-square-foot model train layout in his home. The city of Beverly Hills lists him as one of its "Master Architects." The club was remodeled a number of years ago to reflect a more rustic, less mid-century modern style, but the design structure is so strong that even the antler chandeliers and rustic stonework do not detract from the beauty of the original design and make for a perfect blend of styles. These pictures are by famed architectural photographer Jules Shulman. (Both, GRI.)

THE MONTE CORONA, 1966. The Monte Corona is an interesting complex built in 1966. It is a conference and resort center constructed for the Los Angeles Teachers Association and later sold to the California Teachers Association. It was designed by Frank Coppedge, AIA, of Fleming and Coppedge Architects. In 1975, Calvary Chapel of Costa Mesa purchased the properties for use as a Bible college and conference center. In 1996, the college moved to a larger facility in Murrietta hot springs, and the Twin Peaks facility was renovated and reopened as Calvary Chapel Twin Peaks. The development is organized around a circular central building with radiating A-frame roof surrounded by a concentric semicircular wing of residential units. Its design layout is strikingly similar to nearby condominium project Fernrock Estates, which was built on the site of Caroline Dobbins's Fernrock Ranch. (Both, DW.)

FERNROCK ESTATES, 1970. Also commissioned by the California Teachers Association, the Fernrock Estates condominium development follows a layout similar to that of the Monte Corona, with a central circular recreation building surrounded by two (not one) concentric rows of residential units. The roof pitch on the condos becomes increasingly steep as one moves from the exterior row of units—which almost seem Wrightian in inspiration—to the central recreation building. Even the pool radiates out from the center in a manner similar to that of the conference center. Given the similarities of the two complexes, it is not surprising that Fernrock Estates was also designed by Frank Coppedge. (Above, CD; right, DW.)

COUNTRY CLUB VILLAS, 1966. Renowned Palm Springs mid-century modernist architect William F. Cody, FAIA, also built in Lake Arrowhead. The condos on Grass Valley Road near the country club are part of the vision of what the Lake Arrowhead Development Company had envisioned as part of the new Lake Arrowhead experience. The villas offered two- and three-bedroom units complete with resort amenities such as room service, maid service, continuous exterior maintenance, and golf club and lake privileges, with prices starting at $39,000. In addition to designing many residential and commercial projects in the Palm Springs area, Cody specialized in country clubs and was responsible for the design of the Eldorado Country Club, Tamarisk Country Club, the Racquet Club, the Tennis Club, and the Seven Lakes Clubhouse. (DW.)

CEDAR GLEN FIRE STATION NO. 93, EARLY 1970s. Prominently visible on Highway 173 in Cedar Glen is this unstaffed, glass-sided fire station designed by David Hatfield. It houses specialized equipment such as an ambulance and structure engine. Because the building is glazed on all sides, the equipment is on display and clearly visible from the street. Hatfield was raised in San Bernardino and graduated from the University of California, Berkeley, in 1966. He also taught architecture at San Bernardino Valley for many years. His designs are inspired by the work of Frank Lloyd Wright, Raphael Soriano, and Bruce Goff. He also built his own home starting in 1973; it was located near the base of the mountain. He built it in $100 increments, with the total cost coming in at under $20,000. Much of his designs were experimental, as was his house. (DW.)

ARROCREST RESORT, 1984. Even world-famous architect John Lautner Jr., FAIA, had a commission for a project in Lake Arrowhead. It was a resort that was never built. However, models and renderings exist at the Getty Research Institute. It was to be located in Cedar Glen. Lautner was an apprentice of Frank Lloyd Wright and is most known for his design of the Chemosphere and Silvertop. His most important contribution, however, stems from his influence in the creation of the Googie buildings, which are named after his design of Googie's Coffee Shop in Hollywood. After Lautner graduated from Northern Michigan University, he joined the first class of Frank Lloyd Wright's Talisen Fellows at Spring Green, Wisconsin. This photograph is from the Lautner Archive, Research Library, Getty Research Institute, LA ©2022 The John Lautner Foundation. (LA-GRI.)

Nine

THE MODERNISTS
MORE MID-CENTURY MODERNISM

A NEW STYLE EMERGES. The early 1960s and 1970s became a period of immense growth in Arrowhead. Many new subdivisions opened up in Arrowhead Woods, and many modern cabins were built. In Hamiltair alone, there are a number of interesting modern A-frames from this period. This photograph shows a house designed by W. Keith Duncan in 1968 with a prow-shaped view window under the eaves. (DW.)

AUERBACHER LODGE, 1952. Famed Austrian-American modernist Richard Neutra, FAIA and AIA Gold Medalist, built this house in Running Springs about seven miles east of Lake Arrowhead. He also built another house for the Auerbachers in Redlands which is listed on the National Register of Historic Places. Neutra briefly worked for Frank Lloyd Wright and then with fellow Austrian and architectural school friend Rudolf Schindler when he lived and worked on the Kings Road House in Hollywood, a cooperative live/work space. These photographs are by noted architectural photographer Julius Shulman. (Both, GRI.)

DAVIS HOUSE, 1960. This small house was designed by David Fowler for his mother six years after his graduation from USC. It was photographed by Julius Shulman. Fowler is said to have designed numerous houses in Lake Arrowhead, although their locations are not known. Fowler's most famous house is perhaps another structure he designed for his mother called Ridgetop. It can be seen in the 2001 film *The Fast and the Furious* as the undercover headquarters of the LAPD. That house was torn down in 2002 to make room for what is now the second-largest home in Los Angeles, the Pritzer estate. (Both, GRI.)

Los Angeles Times HOME MAGAZINE

AUGUST 31, 1952

Story on Page 3   *Color photo by George E. Peterson*

THE ARROWHEAD HOME OF CONRAD BUFF, THE ARTIST, AND HIS WIFE MARY, THE AUTHOR, USES THE HEAVY DIAGONALS SUPPORTING THE ROOF TO ACHIEVE THE APPEARANCE OF GREATER SIZE IN A CABIN ONLY 22 FEET HIGH AND 20 FEET WIDE—A CABIN IN COMPLETE HARMONY WITH TREES AND SKY.

Modern Cabins in the Pines

CONRAD BUFF CABIN, 1952. The year architect Conrad Buff graduated from USC, he designed this small cabin for his parents in Lake Arrowhead on 13 wooded acres. It was published in *HOME Magazine* of the *Los Angeles Times* on August 31, 1952. Buff's father, also named Conrad Buff, was a noted artist who, along with his wife, Mary Buff, created a number of illustrated children's books. The Buffs' family friends included many important modernists, including architects Rudolf Schindler and Richard Neutra. Their influence can be seen in the design of this house, with its A-frame structure and built-in furnishings. Buff formed a firm with USC classmate Donald Hensman. Their firm, Buff and Hensman, became known for its work in the case study house program. Unfortunately, it appears that the original two-bedroom cabin no longer exists. A new four-bedroom, 6,086-square-foot house replaced the cabin in 2010. (LAT.)

THE DRAGON CABIN, 1940. Wallace Neff, FAIA, designed an 800-square-foot cabin for opera star Amelita Galli-Curci. It was later purchased by Oscar- and Emmy-winning composer Carmen Dragon and father of Daryl Dragon (the "Captain" of Captain and Tennille), who added an additional 2,000 square feet. Neff designed a total of four houses for Galli-Curci. Neff (a student of Ralph Adams Cram) was most well known for his Spanish Colonial Revival homes, but as any good Period Revival architect, he was able to work in a myriad of styles. He also came up with the design for "bubble" houses—inexpensive, dome-shaped structures built of concrete cast over an inflatable balloon that were popular in Egypt, Brazil, and West Africa in the late 1940s and 1950s. The bubble house concept did not catch on in the United States. Elvis Presley and the Beatles are said to have been guests at the cabin. (DS.)

MITRY LANE CABIN, 1960. Frank Lloyd Wright Jr. was known as Lloyd Wright to distinguish himself from his famous father, Frank Lloyd Wright. He worked as a landscape architect on a number of projects, including the 1915 Panama-California Exposition in San Diego and the second and third bandshells for the Hollywood Bowl. Later, he worked with his father and Rudolph Schindler on the Imperial Hotel in Tokyo and on Barnsdale Park. In 1920, he ventured out on his own, and by 1922, he was a production manager at Paramount Studios designing 12th-century village sets for the Douglas Fairbanks version of *Robin Hood*. His most famous building is the Wayfarer's Chapel in Rancho Palos Verdes, and the largest collection of Lloyd Wright buildings can be found at the Institute of Mentalphysics, located east of Joshua Tree National Park. This is a small cabin he designed near the village on Mitry Lane. Its expressive, organic forms are typical of Lloyd Wright's designs. (DW.)

VENTANAS DEL LAGO, 1965. This house was designed by architect Fred McDowell in 1965. A USC graduate, McDowell briefly worked for Richard Neutra. The house was featured in the *Los Angeles Times HOME Magazine* in 1966. McDowell said, "I want to do something like a boat with prow opening up to the view. So I started with that element and worked backward into the house." Houses with large A-frame gables on all four sides and a floor plan that is rotated 45 degrees under the roof eave are sometimes referred to as Flying-W houses. There are at least a dozen Flying-W houses on the mountain. Interiors were designed by Pat Mayeda, interior designer/artist and member of the Scripps College Fine Arts Foundation. She incorporated accessories designed by members of the Claremont Art Group. The contractor was John Ashton. It was photographed by famed architectural photographer Julius Shulman. A sign in front refers to the house as Ventanas del Lago—Spanish for "lake windows." (DW.)

LEAKY HOUSE, 1966. Built by the same architect who designed the Lake Arrowhead Country Club, Richard Dorman, FAIA, this house overlooking the lake made the cover of the *Los Angeles Times HOME Magazine* for the issue dated July 17, 1966—the same issue that featured Ventana del Lago. What is unusual about the fenestration of this large A-frame window is that there is now central mullion on the window. Although Rudolf Schindler designed the first modern A-frame in Lake Arrowhead in the 1930s, the building type did not become popular until after World War II. It was particularly popular in Lake Arrowhead during the 1960s building boom. Various versions exist, from simple A-frames to much larger houses where the A-frame roof is only the central portion of the house flanked by one or two wings on either side. Often, these houses would have a double-height living room, sometimes sunken, and the window under the A-frame could be curved or come to a point, as at Ventanas del Lago. (LAT.)

FLYING-W HOUSE, 1967. Los Angeles architect John Gerard designed this W-frame house, referred to locally as a Flying-W House, in 1967. Gerard designed a number of houses in the Lake Arrowhead area, and at least one other is also a Flying-W. Flying-W houses were popular in Arrowhead from the mid- to late 1960s and are so named because the W form of the roof appears to be ready to fly away. (LG.)

FERBER HOUSE, 1968. Michael Black, AIA, was a prominent Palm Springs mid-century modernist who trained at USC. Black was responsible for many mid-century buildings in the Palm Springs area. He also taught design at SCIArc (Southern California Institute of Architecture). He designed this getaway cabin for his family in 1968. It has over 100 windows so that one can see the forest from almost any angle in the house. It was featured in *TIME Magazine* in 1971. Bernie Kerkvlite of Skyline Ponds recently redid the landscaping, enhancing the indoor/outdoor connection of the original design. The current owner calls it his utopian retreat. (Both, DW.)

LIBERACE HOUSE, 1973. Here is a photograph of Liberace getting the keys to his boat from Wilmer Jaun, manager of the Lake Arrowhead marinas. Liberace's home in Hamiltair Estates had candelabras marking the entrance. Although the building CCNRs state that the house be French Norman, this was the 1970s, and quite a few liberties were taken in its interpretation. Like many mountain houses, it had a great room with an open beam ceiling and an open beam ceiling in the principal bedroom with a signature chandelier. The kitchen also had a beamed ceiling and custom tile mural with persimmon-colored field tiles. In true 1970s fashion, the bathroom sported flocked wallpaper, and two large carved lions flanked the living room fireplace. The sliding glass doors that opened to the lakefront terrace were surrounded by stylized Gothic arches. The house was built by contractor John Bueller. (Above, RK; below, DV.)

EAGLE POINT, 1981. In 1981, former Ice Follies star Carol Probst and her husband, Walter, built a new 11,919-square-foot house on Eagle Point. The house was designed as a showplace with entertainment in mind; the Probsts hosted numerous dignitaries, including Bob and Dolores Hope and Pres. Gerald Ford. All of them stayed in the Blue Suite, a guest suite so named for its blue silk wallpaper and blue onyx fireplace. Carolyn and Walter also founded and built the Lake Arrowhead Ice Castle international training center in 1988, bringing Olympic-caliber skating to the mountain. The house features large two-story windows overlooking the lake, including in the bathroom. The walk-in tub and shower featured a sequined shower curtain that the family affectionately dubbed the Liberace bathroom for all the glitz the bathroom exuded. The interiors have been described as "retro Austin Powers décor" for the extensive use of Lucite, including a circular chrome and Lucite stair. The house, which is situated on Eagle Point and has large expanses of glass, features spectacular views of the lake. San Francisco–based Taylor-Huston Architects designed the house. (CF.)

THE JONES HOUSE, 1990. Thirty-seven years after Conrad Buff built a house for his parents with his college classmate and partner Donald Hensman, their firm built another house in Lake Arrowhead, this one being much larger than the small cabin. Buff and Hensman's early work was much lighter post-and-beam construction, while their later work (as featured here) is far more substantial and has a heavier feel. Buff and Hensman later joined with Calvin Straub to form Buff, Straub, and Hensman, which became known for the firm's participation in the Case Study Program, where they designed Case Study Houses No. 20 and No. 28. Case Study House No. 20 is sometimes considered the firm's masterpiece, with its plywood vaulting and factory-produced stressed skin panels. Buff, Straub, and Hensman were all Fellows of the American Institute of Architects—an honor reserved for the top 3 percent of those in the profession. (MSP.)

Ten

THE DREAMERS
FANTASY, ROMANCE,
AND OLD ARROWHEAD

SANTA'S VILLAGE AND A RETURN OF OLD ARROWHEAD STYLE. The 1950s and 1960s are sometimes referred to as the Golden Age of Fantasy. The Disney movies *Cinderella*, *Peter Pan*, and *Robin Hood* all were made in the early 1950s. The horrors of World War II had people wishing to escape to a more magical time, and the prosperity after the war made it possible to build one's dreams. Cinderella houses became a thing, as did the development of theme parks. Arrowhead was no exception. Still others wished to simply continue the traditions of prewar Arrowhead. (JL.)

CINDERELLA HOUSES. "Cinderella houses" came into fashion in Southern California during the early 1950s; the first was designed and built by Jean Vandruff in Downey in 1953. This fantasy variation of a California ranch house became popular all over Southern California in places such as the San Fernando Valley, Orange County, Santa Barbara, and beyond. Perhaps the most elaborate of the Cinderella houses can be found in San Luis Obispo at the Madonna Inn. With its widespread popularity, it is no surprise that Cinderella houses can also be found in Lake Arrowhead. A steep gabled entry over the front door can be found in one version, as well as applied gingerbread trim and shutters often painted in a contrasting color to accentuate its decorative quality. Another example of a Cinderella house can be seen in the Storybook Inn in Skyforest, with its decorative wooden shutters and gingerbread trim. (DW.)

SANTA'S VILLAGE, 1955. Six weeks before Disneyland opened, Glen Holland, a Crestline resident, opened Santa's Village on land leased from the Henck family. Led by Putty Henck, general contractor, a team of local artisans and craftsman created the whimsical Santa's Village. Holland went on to open two more Santa's Villages—one in Dundee, Illinois, and another in Santa Cruz, California. It was the first franchised theme park in the world. When the franchise went bankrupt in the 1970s, ownership reverted to the Henck family. They expanded the park, introducing more rides, horseback riding, and a Fantasy Forest with nature trails. In 1998, the Henck family sold the park. After extensive work and restoration, the new owners reopened Santa's Village in 2016 as an outdoor adventure park named SkyPark Santa's Village. (Both, JL.)

FAMILY NEST, 1998. This was designed by the author for her family in 1998, when she was in partnership with FSW Architects. The design, true to Arrowhead style, is eclectic, incorporating elements of French Norman design, Craftsman architecture, and fin-de-siècle Northern European design. The front facade was inspired by buildings in Normandy combined with an eyebrow window—a nod to the family's Polish heritage. The interior finish harkens back to a craftsman aesthetic. The colors and materials mimic the colors and textures of the forest, and interior finishes include the use of Batchelder Tile and Art Glass. The house has two main facades—the street facade, which is shown above, and the lake facade shown at left. The lake facade has a tower modeled after the tower designed by Finnish architect Eliel Saarinen on the 1904 Soor-Meriioki Villa in Leningrad Oblast. (Both, DW.)

CHÂTEAU ENCHANTÉ, 2000. This property once owned by Beach Boy Brian Wilson (and reputed to have also been owned by Disney's Michael Eisner) is situated on a prominent point across from Lake Arrowhead Village. At one point, it was referred to as Château Enchanté, but it is not clear if the current owners still refer to the house by that name. It is a striking example of the work of designer Dave Abbott. Abbott gained popularity during the late 1900s and early 2000s for his fanciful, storybook French Norman designs replete with extensive detailing and half-timbering both inside and out. This is just one example of the many houses he designed in Arrowhead. Abbott passed away in 2020, but the legacy of his many projects in the Arrowhead area will live on as a continuation of the Old Arrowhead style first introduced by McNeal Swasey in 1922. (DW.)

CEDAR HOLLOW (ABOVE) AND TOAD'S COTTAGE (LEFT), EARLY 2000s. These two projects represent the versatility of designer/ builder Ron Dolman. Toad's Cottage is a delightful smaller home built in Skyforest that expresses the elements of whimsy on a personal scale. Dolman's design skills are evident as he manages to keep the personal aspect of design on a much larger scale in his later design of Cedar Hollow. One enters Cedar Hollow thru a gatehouse and over a bridge (not shown) to a refuge tucked away in a cedar hollow that would be equally at home in England or France. (Both, MSP.)

WEST SHORE HOUSE, 2005. This small house was commissioned for a lakefront parcel in North Bay but was never built. The client had wanted a design that harkened back to the Golden Age of Arrowhead's architecture in the 1920s and 1930s. The design incorporated steep roofs and an entry tower typical of Norman architecture. The architect, Michael Burch, FAIA, is internationally known for his traditional residential work, having exhibited four times at La Biennale di Venezia in Venice, Italy, and the only Southern California architect to have won three Palladio Awards, the only national design award given for excellence in traditional design. (DW.)

TARALOCH, 2006. Designed by Dave Abbot with Ron Dolman, this house is a fanciful play on the Old Arrowhead Style, complete with half-timbering, turrets on the roof, stonework, and a circular tower. It replaced a small house built in 1946 for J.W. "Chick" Merrick and later owned by comedian Red Skelton. Merrick first built a house next door in 1929. That house has also been demolished and replaced by a much larger house. (PP.)

ARROWHEAD POINTE, 2007. This 11,000-square-foot house was designed for illustrator Glen Keane and his wife. It replaced a much smaller house on the property designed by architect Reginald Johnson, FAIA, that had been published in *Architectural Digest* in 1934. Exceptional attention to detail can be found throughout the new house. Of note is the stonework crafted by a local Arrowhead stone carver, a native of Stuttgart, Marcel Mächler, who is said to have worked on the restoration of the Notre Dame Cathedral prior to it burning. The architect, Richardson Robertson III, specializes in traditional residential design and is internationally recognized for his work. Both the owner and the architect gave careful consideration to the implications of tearing down the original house, but ultimately, the decision was made to create a new structure respectful of the architectural tradition of the area. The new house portrays a convincing interpretation of an authentic French Norman structure. (Both, GK.)

THE HAMPTON HOUSE, 2008. At 16,400 square feet and with a 23-car garage, this 10-bedroom, 16-bathroom house is Lake Arrowhead's second-largest lakefront property. The design is a bit unusual for Lake Arrowhead, as it is more reminiscent of a Hampton seaside resort home, but the rock-faced first floor, slate roof, and tower make it stylistically compatible with Old Arrowhead houses. The house takes advantage of its large lakefront view, and most rooms open up to expansive views down the lake—some of the most extensive anywhere on the lake. Since the house is located in a gated area, the public facade faces the lake. (Both, DV.)

TOTEM POLE LODGE, 1923. Designed by McNeal Swasey for Charles M. Hackley, this house is one of the early lakefront properties in Lake Arrowhead. Hackley was the son of Charles H. Hackley, who made his fortune in the lumber business. Charles M. Hackley lost his eyesight dynamiting tree stumps on his farm. Shown here is the dock with ropes around the perimeter to prevent Charles from falling into the lake. In spite of his disability, he remained active and was an avid equestrian. (DW.)

TOTEM POLE LODGE REMODEL, 2008. In 2008, Totem Pole Lodge was extensively remodeled by architect John Lyles, AIA. Lyles states that his work is inspired by Arrowhead's traditional architecture and the architecture of great Western lodges, especially Bernard Maybeck's early work. There is a high level of craftsmanship throughout the new addition that seamlessly blends with the original structure. (JL.)

HIDDEN CREEK, 2007. The book ends with the design of the Pine Rose Cabins wedding venue designed by owners David and Tricia Dufour with Bernie Kerkvliet of Skyline Ponds. The romantic vision of the Victorians on the mountain has come alive once again with one-of-a-kind crafted structures similar in spirit to the structures found at Pinecrest over 100 years earlier. That vision includes a beautiful custom log-and-branch gazebo and grounds incorporating streams and ponds enhanced with native plants. Pine Rose Cabins Resort consists of cabins spread over a 10-acre site in Twin Peaks, some of which date back to the early 1900s. The current owners purchased the property in 1993 and developed the resort into what it is today—a romantic forest dreamland for couples starting out on their life's journey together, as captured by photographer James Tang in these photographs. (Both, JT.)

INDEX

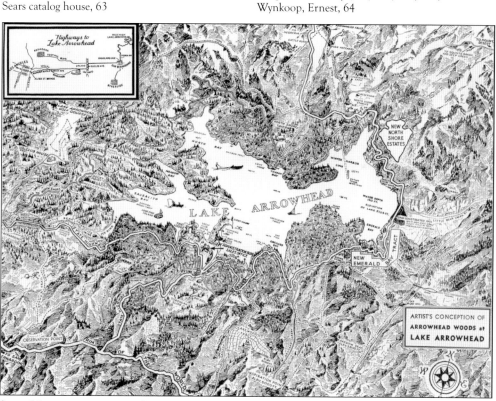

SALES MAP FROM THE 1930S SHOWING POINTS OF INTEREST.

DISCOVER THOUSANDS OF LOCAL HISTORY BOOKS
FEATURING MILLIONS OF VINTAGE IMAGES

Arcadia Publishing, the leading local history publisher in the United States, is committed to making history accessible and meaningful through publishing books that celebrate and preserve the heritage of America's people and places.

Find more books like this at
www.arcadiapublishing.com

Search for your hometown history, your old stomping grounds, and even your favorite sports team.

Consistent with our mission to preserve history on a local level, this book was printed in South Carolina on American-made paper and manufactured entirely in the United States. Products carrying the accredited Forest Stewardship Council (FSC) label are printed on 100 percent FSC-certified paper.

MADE IN THE